ONE MINUTE WITH THE MEN OF THE BIBLE

JIM GEORGE

HARVEST HOUSE PUBLISHERS
EUGENE, OREGON

Cover by Bryce Williamson

One Minute with the Men of the Bible
Copyright © 2018 Jim George
Published by Harvest House Publishers
Eugene, Oregon 97408
www.harvesthousepublishers.com

ISBN 978-0-7369-7360-1 (Milano Softone™)
ISBN 978-0-7369-7361-8 (eBook)

Library of Congress Cataloging-in-Publication Data is on file at the Library of Congress, Washington, DC.

Printed in China

18 19 20 21 22 23 24 25 26 / RDS-SK / 10 9 8 7 6 5 4 3 2 1

Contents

Section 1: Old Testament Men

Section 2: New Testament Men

Section 3: Jesus, the Greatest Man Who Ever Lived

OLD TESTAMENT MEN

A Man Who Was a Weak Leader

*You [Moses] shall speak to him [Aaron]
and put the words in his mouth.*

EXODUS 4:15

God called Aaron to be Moses's spokesman to the leadership of the children of Israel and to the king of Egypt. This was a great honor, and initially Aaron did his job well. But somewhere in all that was going on, Aaron became a man lost in the shadow of Moses, one of the greatest Bible characters of all time. Even though Aaron was a coleader in the mass exodus and often stood shoulder to shoulder with Moses against the rebellion of the people, he never seemed to be a central or essential figure. His greatest moments were as a follower. And tragically, the two times when he did stand alone as a leader, he showed himself to be weak. (See the incident with the golden calf in Exodus 32, and the time when he and Miriam questioned their brother Moses's leadership in Numbers 12.)

What lessons can you learn from the life of Aaron?

Examine yourself often for areas of weakness. Make an honest assessment of your strengths and weaknesses. Seek out those who can help you avoid situations you cannot handle on your own.

Form strong convictions. Because Aaron lacked strong convictions, he caved in to the ungodly requests of the people. Establish your biblical guidelines. Then, fortified with God's answers, you will be willing and able to stand when asked to make a "golden calf."

Failure does not disqualify you from service. Aaron failed both God and Moses on numerous occasions, yet God still used Aaron in significant ways.

Be a faithful follower. Aaron was envious of Moses's leadership and, together with his sister, challenged Moses's authority. The Bible tells you to obey your leaders. Obedience starts with being a faithful follower. You can never be a good leader until you are a good follower.

Learn from your mistakes and ask for God's wisdom so you make fewer mistakes in the future.

A Man Who Gave an Acceptable Offering

Abel also brought of the firstborn of his flock…
And the LORD respected Abel and his offering.

GENESIS 4:4

The second son of Adam and Eve, Abel was the younger brother of Cain. When the brothers offered sacrifices, God was pleased with Abel's but was not pleased with Cain's. Out of jealousy, Cain murdered Abel in cold blood. Abel died for obediently offering to God what was acceptable, and he lives forever as an example of righteousness and faith (Hebrews 11:4).

Our devotion to God is measured by the offerings we bring to Him and the heart attitude behind them. We don't know why Cain's offering was unacceptable, but we do know that his response to God's rejection showed Cain's true heart. Abel, on the other hand, possessed a heart of faith and a deep respect for God. He gladly offered God the very best he had to give. To God, this was pleasing and acceptable, and He gave this testimony in Hebrews 11:4: "By faith Abel offered to God a more excellent sacrifice than Cain, through which he obtained witness that he was righteous, God testifying of his gifts…"

When you give—whether it is your time, your energy, your possessions, or your money—ask yourself a few questions. Am I giving my best? Am I giving with a joyful heart? Am I giving because I have to or because I want to? What am I withholding from God?

No one can out give God, so give from your heart, and give liberally. "God loves a cheerful giver" (2 Corinthians 9:7). And don't worry or hold back: "God is able to make all grace abound toward you, that you, always having all sufficiency in all things, may have an abundance for every good work" (verse 8).

A Man Who Obeyed God

[Abraham] believed in the LORD,
and He accounted it to him for righteousness.
GENESIS 15:6

Abraham (which means "father of a multitude") is one of the most important figures in the Bible. He was the first of the patriarchs (Abraham, Isaac, and Jacob), the father of the Israelite nation, from which came the Jewish people. Known initially as Abram (meaning "exalted father"), God told him to leave his own country and go to an undisclosed land, where He promised Abraham would become a great nation and be a blessing to all the families of the earth. How did Abraham respond to this perplexing order? He took his wife, Sarah, and left all that he had known to follow God into the unknown (see Genesis 11:26–17:5; Nehemiah 9:7).

Another promise God made to Abraham was that of a son from his barren wife, Sarah—a son who would produce nations and kings. For 25 years Abraham waited for the promised son. At last, through a miracle, Isaac—meaning "laughter"—was born! God, as always, faithfully fulfilled His promise (see Genesis 17:15-19).

Abraham was a man who obeyed God. He had been told to leave his country and go to an unknown land, and he did it. Along the way, Abraham was told where to go and what to do, and he did it. What is your level of obedience to God? How compliant are you to His commands and instructions?

If you are having a problem with doing what God asks, expects, and requires, acknowledge your weakness. Act to exercise and strengthen the muscle of obedience in the little things. Then, when some seemingly impossible challenge comes along, you can respond as Abraham did. You can quickly, quietly, and without question obey God.

God's blessing awaited Abraham on the other side of every act of obedience. And the same will be true for you. Don't miss out on God's blessings by not obeying Him.

A Man Who Had Great Faith

He [Abraham] believed in the LORD,
and He accounted it to him for righteousness.

GENESIS 15:6

Nearly 100 times in the Bible God is referred to as the "God of Abraham," or Abraham is referred to as the "father" of the Hebrew people. Abraham was told by God to leave his country and go to another land. Later God made an earth-shattering promise: a son would be born to Sarah, Abraham's wife, and the son would produce nations, kings, and peoples. From that promise came the Messiah, Jesus Christ.

Abraham is revered by the Jewish people, but he is also a significant illustration for the Christian understanding that salvation is by faith in Jesus and not in religious activity. The apostle Paul spoke of Abraham's faith in several of his epistles (Romans 4; Galatians 3). Paul explained that Abraham was saved by his faith in God: Abraham "believed God, and it was accounted to him for righteousness" (Galatians 3:6).

Faith—saving faith—gave Abraham his security and assurance. Abraham believed that God would protect him and fulfill His promises. How about you? Do you possess Abraham's kind of saving faith? Without Abraham's kind of faith, "it is impossible to please Him, for he who comes to God must believe that He is, and that He is a rewarder of those who diligently seek Him" (Hebrews 11:6).

You can experience Abraham's saving faith by diligently seeking God through His Son, Jesus Christ. "That by the name of Jesus Christ…there is no other name under heaven given among men by which we must be saved" (Acts 4:10-12). Life will take on new meaning when your faith rests in Jesus and, like Abraham, you live in God's saving grace.

A Man Who Had an Eye for Gold

I have sinned against the LORD…
I saw…silver…gold…
I coveted them and I took them.

JOSHUA 7:20-21

Achan was a soldier in the Israelite army that defeated the large city-state of Jericho. He and a much-smaller force were next sent to Ai, where, to the horror of the people, the army was defeated and 36 men were killed in battle. God said the reason for the defeat was that "Israel has sinned." Through God's guidance, the soldier Achan was singled out as the reason for the defeat. The name *Achan* means "troublesome," and this man truly lived up to the meaning of his name by coveting the spoils of war that were to be offered to God. Because of his selfish desires for worldly goods, the army was defeated and 36 men had been killed. As punishment, Achan and all his family and goods were destroyed.

Living in a materialistic society offers many temptations. And like Achan, you might assume that succumbing to one or more of these temptations would not be a big deal. After all, no one will see what you are doing and if no one gets hurt, then it's okay! But like Achan, your actions will always affect others, starting with your relationship with God. The apostle John gives this caution and admonishment: "For all that is in the world—the lust of the flesh, the lust of the eyes, and the pride of life—is not of the Father but is of the world. And the world is passing away, and the lust of it; but he who does the will of God abides forever" (1 John 2:16-17).

God does not miss a thing. Your actions never go unnoticed, and every sin has its consequences. Rather than focusing on the world and its temporary allurements, keep your eyes on God, His blessings, and the eternal reward that is waiting for you in heaven.

A Man Who Worked

Have dominion over…every living thing that moves on the earth.

GENESIS 1:28

Rumor has it that work is one of the consequences of the fall of man—that if Adam had not eaten that apple, we wouldn't have to work. But the truth is that work existed before the fall. Long before Adam, we witness God at work in the creation of the universe. God modeled for all, and forever, the inherent dignity of work. Then God did one final creative act—He "created man in His own image" and sent Adam to work in the Garden of Eden. Unfortunately, Adam's fall into sin brought with it a curse for all mankind: Our work will be hard and difficult! As God said to Adam, "In the sweat of your face you shall eat bread" (Genesis 3:19).

Throughout the Bible, work is seen as a normal and natural part of life. The book of Proverbs has a lot to say about work. For instance: "In all labor there is profit, but idle chatter leads only to poverty" (Proverbs 14:23). Even Jesus, the Son of God in human flesh, worked as a carpenter (Mark 6:3). And the apostle Paul worked long hours as a tentmaker when he was not preaching.

Clearly, work is not bad—it is not a result of sin. So how should you view work?

- View your work as a calling from God. As you do your work, you have the opportunity to bring honor to Him (Matthew 5:16).

- View your work as beneficial. It benefits your family financially (1 Timothy 5:8), and it also produces a healthy mental attitude in you.

- View your work as being done unto the Lord. "Whatever you do, do it heartily, as to the Lord and not to men…for you serve the Lord Christ" (Colossians 3:23-24).

- View your work as a way to represent Christ—as part of being "ambassadors for Christ" (2 Corinthians 5:20).

A Man Who Was First

God created man in His own image;
in the image of God He created him.
GENESIS 1:27

Adam, whose name means "mankind," was the world's first man and he was perfect in every way. God formed Adam from the dust of the ground and put him in the Garden of Eden to tend and keep it. God also put trees in the garden—including the tree of life and the tree of the knowledge of good and evil. God then told Adam he could eat freely from every tree of the garden except the tree of the knowledge of good and evil. If he ate of that tree, then he would die.

Adam disobeyed God and, along with Eve, ate of the forbidden fruit. As a result, sin spread to all mankind (Romans 5:12). But God came to Adam and Eve's rescue and salvaged their lives. He killed animals to cover and clothe their naked bodies. He then sent them out of the garden so they would not eat of the tree of life and experience perpetual death. He also pointed them toward a glorious solution for their sin—a Savior for mankind (Genesis 3:15).

The life of Adam gives us a glimpse of what God originally intended for mankind—a perfect relationship with Him in a perfect environment of health and peace. Unfortunately, the first Adam disobeyed God and lost his relationship with his creator. But thankfully, the new Adam, Jesus Christ, also known as the "last Adam," came to earth to restore that lost relationship with God.

Are you experiencing God's grace through the "last Adam," Jesus Christ (1 Corinthians 15:45)? If so, you are presently living in a relationship with God that will one day be permanently realized in heaven, that perfect place where, once again, all things will be perfect.

A Man Who Played the Blame Game

Ahab said to [Elijah],
"Is that you, O troubler of Israel?"
1 KINGS 18:17

Ahab was the eighth king of Israel, the northern kingdom, and he reigned 22 years in Samaria. His wife was Jezebel, a heathen princess from Phoenicia. As a result of her evil influence, the storm god, Baal-Melcarth, became the established deity of worship. Ahab built a temple to honor this pagan god. Baal worship became so strong it appeared that the knowledge of the true God would be lost. God raised up Elijah to oppose Ahab and proclaimed a three-year drought as punishment for the country's apostasy.

At the end of the three years, Elijah confronted Ahab, who immediately blamed Elijah for the drought, calling him "O troubler of Israel." Elijah rightly directed the blame back on Ahab and responded, "I have not troubled Israel, but you and your father's house have, in that you have forsaken the commandments of the LORD and have followed the Baals" (1 Kings 18:18). Even with

God's intervention on several occasions, Ahab continued to be unresponsive to God's warnings through Elijah and continued to blame others for his problems.

How are you to respond to the advice and admonition of others, especially those closest to you and who know you best? Do you humbly accept their counsel and strive to make proper changes, or do you play the "blame game"? When you are confronted for wrong actions and attitudes, do you start blaming others rather than admit your own wrongdoing? Rather than blame others, you are to be "submitting to one another in the fear of God" (Ephesians 5:21).

The Bible gives you this advice: "Without counsel, plans go awry, but in the multitude of counselors they are established" (Proverbs 15:22). Accept God's counsel from His Word, especially when it is offered by those who know and love you. God and your Christian friends want only what's best for you and your Christian testimony.

A Man Who Was a Reluctant Leader

Barak said to her, "If you will go with me,
then I will go;
but if you will not go with me, I will not go!"

JUDGES 4:8

Deborah, a prophetess and judge in Israel, summoned Barak to fight against a vastly superior Canaanite force. Deborah told Barak that God would go before him, and would even defeat this enemy. This was Barak's big chance to lead an army into battle and clinch victory! Unfortunately, rather than be a general, Barak became a lieutenant when he declined Deborah's offer to lead. Deborah then proceeded to make all the command decisions and Barak became a follower. God rebuked Barak's cowardice by the pledge that a woman would slay the Canaanite general Sisera. As predicted, the woman Jael killed the great Canaanite general with a tent peg and a hammer (see Judges 4).

We will never know what might have happened if Barak had stepped up and taken command of the army. The outcome had been predicted, but Barak's opportunity for victory was lost because of his unwillingness to lead.

As a Christian man, God gives you the opportunity—and responsibility—to lead. God is asking you to lead your family. He has also gifted you for service, which can open the door for opportunities to lead in your local church. And as a Christian, you may find opportunities to lead in your workplace or community.

Barak was afraid to lead, so Deborah had to lead by default. How about you? Are you failing to lead in your family, leaving your wife to lead by default? You may have the abilities and gifts to lead in your church, but are you choosing to sit on the sidelines and let others lead by default? Rest assured that God will go with you and give you whatever is needed to be a leader in your home and elsewhere. Don't decline God's offer to lead. Step up to the challenge!

A Man Who Was Kind

*You have comforted me, and have spoken kindly
to your maidservant,
though I am not like one of your maidservants.*
RUTH 2:13

When you think of the qualities that describe a man's man, a leader's leader, or a man of stature, "kindness" would not be on most men's list. In today's culture, we are taught that masculinity means being macho and in charge, being the strong and silent type, and showing little or no mercy or kindness.

But this image of a man is contrary to God's design. God's man walks by the Spirit and exhibits kindness. He is to be kindly affectionate, and to be kind to others. Jesus Himself possessed meekness and gentleness. These qualities were also exhibited by the man Boaz.

Beginning in Ruth chapter 2, we see Boaz displaying many acts of kindness. He greeted his workers with kind words. He showed kindness and mercy by asking Ruth about her situation and providing grain for her and her widowed mother-in-law, Naomi. His most significant act of kindness was to provide a home for Ruth and Naomi.

Genuine kindness cannot be manufactured. It is to be your response to God's saving love through Jesus Christ. God is calling you, as one of His men, to demonstrate real and sincere love that goes far beyond pretense and politeness. God's kindness is love in action. It means looking for ways to express Christ's love to others. Jesus said that even when you give a cup of water in His name you are performing an act of kindness (Matthew 10:42).

If you are having a problem showing kindness, start reading through the Gospels and underline the many acts of kindness performed by our Lord. He is your model. And guess what? Boaz, another model of godliness and kindness, was in the genealogical line of Jesus Christ, the Messiah!

A Man Who Had Valor

There was…a man of great wealth,
  of the family of Elimelech.
His name was Boaz.

RUTH 2:1

Too often we hear that "chivalry is dead." Chivalry describes the actions and attitudes of a man toward women, which includes being courteous, generous, and noble in character. In other words, chivalry describes a man of valor. In our society, where the distinctions between men and women are being vigorously erased, it is easy to stand aside, drop any idea of chivalry, and treat women as "one of the guys." If you are married and not careful, you may even find yourself treating your wife with less than the honor God requires: "Husbands, likewise, dwell with them with understanding, giving honor to the wife, as to the weaker vessel" (1 Peter 3:7).

Chivalry and valor may be lacking in our society, but we find them on display in Boaz's life, which serves as a model of what valor looks like. Here are a few of the qualities of valor that describe Boaz and provide a model for Christian men today.

- *Noble.* Boaz is described as "a man of great wealth," which can also be translated "man of valor." Boaz was diligent and amassed wealth, but not at the expense of his character.
- *Friendly.* Boaz greeted his workers with warmth, and even welcomed the stranger named Ruth when she came to glean in his field.
- *Encouraging.* Boaz pointed out Ruth's strong qualities and spoke of them to affirm her.

Compared to other religions, one of the distinctives of Christianity is that it gives women a special place of honor. Chivalry and valor may be dead in our society, but as a Christian man, you can value and appreciate women the way He does. Treat women as special, starting with your mother, wife, and daughters. Be a man of valor, and you will provide a model for your sons and others to follow.

A Man Who Brought an Inferior Offering

Cain brought an offering…
but [God] did not respect Cain
* and his offering.*

GENESIS 4:4-5

Two brothers, Cain and Abel, ushered in the world's first "second generation." When Eve gave birth to Cain, she may have thought he was the promised Savior referred to in Genesis 3:15. Sadly, she later learned that was not the case. Cain murdered Abel, and in the New Testament, his name is used to represent those who do not possess the new birth in Christ and are the children of the devil, lovers of evil, and children of the wicked one (1 John 3:12). Cain did not love God nor his brother.

Cain and his poor relationship with God and his brother Abel is a sobering study because it demonstrates the age-old ongoing struggle between right and wrong, good and evil. There are two ways of living—God's way or man's way. And there are two destinies that result from a person's choices and lifestyle—acceptance or rejection by God.

What else do we learn from Cain?

- When you worship God, a proper attitude is mandatory. The fact Cain became angry after his sacrifice had been rejected by God revealed his true heart condition. God rejected both his attitude and his offering.

- The opportunity to do what is right is available at all times. God confronted Cain and his attitude, and gave him the opportunity to repent. Tragically, with an evil, unrepentant heart, he chose to kill his brother.

- Sin is always lurking nearby, but it can be mastered. God warned Cain, "Sin lies at the door. And its desire is for you, but you should rule over it" (Genesis 4:7).

- Uncontrolled anger is a sinful emotion that usually leads to sinful actions. "Cain rose up against Abel his brother and killed him" (Genesis 4:8).

- Anger accompanied by evil actions never achieves God's righteous plans.

- There are always consequences to wrong choices.

A Man Who Saw No Problems

Caleb quieted the people before Moses, and said,
"Let us go up at once and take possession,
for we are well able to overcome it."

NUMBERS 13:30

No problem was too big for Caleb. He knew that God would help him get through each dilemma that came his way. He held this conviction when he first went into the Promised Land as a spy, and 45 years later he still believed it.

We first meet Caleb at age 40 when he was assigned to serve as one of the twelve spies sent by Moses to explore Canaan, the land God had promised to Israel. But when the spies returned, ten of them announced the inability of Israel to overcome the people of the land, who lived in walled cities and had great strength and stature. Caleb and Joshua were the only two who believed that God could give them victory. Because of the unbelief of the people, only Caleb and Joshua were allowed to enter Canaan 40 years later. Then after five years of conquest in the Promised Land, at the age of 85 Caleb tackled and defeated the "great and fortified" city of Hebron (Joshua 14:6-15).

Do you view life as full of impossible problems with no solutions and only defeat? Or do you see obstacles as opportunities for God to show Himself strong on your behalf? God wants you to successfully overcome life's trials and troubles, but to do this you must look to God and follow His advice: "This Book of the Law shall not depart from your mouth, but you shall meditate in it day and night, that you may observe to do according to all that is written in it. For then...you will have good success" (Joshua 1:8).

Caleb believed in God and His ability to see him through any problem. Do as God told Joshua, and read and obey His Word. Stay close to God, and He will stay close to you. Trust Him to see you through all your difficulties, both big and small.

A Man Who Was Morally Upright

The governors and satraps sought to find some charge against Daniel concerning the kingdom; but they could find no charge or fault, because he was faithful; nor was there any error or fault found in him.

DANIEL 6:4

Daniel (which means "God is my judge") was just a teenager from the southern kingdom of Judah when he was taken captive to Babylon by King Nebuchadnezzar in 605 BC.

Even as a young man, Daniel was righteous and avoided any kind of compromise. Because of his moral integrity and God-given wisdom, he was placed in high positions in the Babylonian and Persian governments. Daniel also became a trusted interpreter of dreams. Not only did he make sense of King Nebuchadnezzar's dreams, but he also interpreted the mysterious handwriting that appeared on a wall and predicted King Belshazzar's fall.

Daniel maintained a steadfast commitment to God in a faraway, pagan land. He remains well known as a man who was faithful to God even when his life was threatened and he was cast into a lions' den (Daniel 6:18-24).

What are you like when no one is watching? Integrity keeps you true to a standard at all times. For a Christian man, that standard is the Word of God, and Daniel is a prime example of the impact of integrity. Like Daniel, when your enemies are looking for ways to discredit you and your faith, your integrity will guard you against their attacks. Integrity is what will keep you totally committed to God despite the pressures and temptations that come with living and working within secular and unbelieving societies.

Daniel provides an inspiring model of moral uprightness and how to stand up for God and His purposes in a secular world. Follow Daniel's example. Commit yourself to knowing more of God's Word and standing up for truth and righteousness. Faithfully serve those in authority over you. Pray regularly. Be willing to suffer for God. Follow God in these ways and, like Daniel, be faithful. Your integrity will make a difference in your relationships, your community, and beyond.

A Man Who Had Convictions

*Daniel purposed in his heart
that he would not defile himself
with the portion of the king's delicacies,
nor with the wine which he drank.*

DANIEL 1:8

As a teenager, Daniel was brutally abducted from his homeland and forced into a training program designed to prepare him and other young men for service in the Babylonian government. Without any hope of returning to Jerusalem, it would have been easy for Daniel to give in to the pressure to eat the food and drink the wine that would have defiled his religion, but he didn't! Instead, he wisely gave a counterproposal to the authorities and asked for a test. God honored Daniel's convictions and he was allowed to continue practicing his Jewish dietary habits (Daniel 1:1-19). Here are two lessons about conviction we can learn from the life of Daniel:

The importance of not straying from biblical convictions. Even as a teen, Daniel had developed firm guidelines about his dietary habits. These early convictions set the course for the next 70-plus years of Daniel's life. Do you have a set of godly convictions? If not, you may be setting yourself up for spiritual defeat. Read your Bible. God's Word will help you develop your own set of biblical convictions. They are a must for a man who desires to live a victorious Christian life!

A life of conviction develops courage. Daniel's courage didn't just happen as he was thrust into the lions' den. Rather, it came from a lifetime of trusting God with every aspect of his life. You may not be facing a literal lions' den, but your faith is challenged daily. Strengthen your faith by prayerfully and boldly living out your Christian beliefs. With each and every challenge, God will develop and strengthen your convictions, and this, in turn, will give you the courage to live each day for Him. Your convictions will supply the strength and resolve you need to resist temptation and experience stability in times of uncertainty.

A Man Who Made Prayer a Habit

Daniel...knelt down on his knees three times that day, and prayed and gave thanks before his God, as was his custom since early days.

DANIEL 6:10

As a youth of 16 or 17, Daniel was devout in his religious practices, which included habitual prayer. Alone in a foreign land, Daniel, as a teen, went to prayer to ask God to protect the lives of his three friends from the wrath of King Nebuchadnezzar. Then, 65 years and two world empires later, Daniel found himself looking into the eyes of a den full of hungry lions. Daniel's life was in danger because of his habit of kneeling three times a day in front of an open window to pray to God (Daniel 6:10). He was condemned to death for this.

When Daniel was in his eighties, he read a manuscript from the prophet Jeremiah that predicted that the 70 years of captivity for the Jews was almost over. In response, Daniel did what he had always done: He humbly came before God and, with a heartfelt plea, asked God to honor His decree to return the Jews to their homeland (Daniel 9:1-19). An unwavering commitment to God, nurtured by habitual prayer, sustained and strengthened Daniel to successfully resist the world's temptations and threats.

Take a few lessons from Daniel. His commitment to prayer was a heart commitment. He not only desired to pray, but he was dedicated to prayer and established a time and a place to pray. He was faithful to follow through, no matter what the cost.

Daniel's life illustrates the correlation between a person's prayer life and his public life. If you are presently praying on a regular basis, your commitment to God and His standards will be further strengthened. If prayer is not a habit for you, don't wait. Begin developing the habit of daily prayer so you are ready when difficulties come. The world needs more Daniels—men who possess remarkable character because they are men of habitual prayer.

A Man Who Had a Problem with Pride

Now go…count the people,
that I may know the number of the people.

2 SAMUEL 24:2

David, like many leaders, had a problem with pride. We see this when David decided to take a census and number his army. Even Joab, David's general, who was not a very godly man, thought doing this was a bad idea. God had not sanctioned this census. David either wanted to glory in the size of his military, or wanted to mobilize his troops to acquire more land than God had granted. Whatever the reason, what David did was wrong. As it turned out, the final count was more than one million men! This was an amazingly large army for such a small country.

Rather than trust God, David was ready to trust in the size of his fighting force. As with all sin, there was a consequence. Proverbs 16:18 warns us, "Pride goes before destruction, and a haughty spirit before a fall." David's pride not only hurt himself, but also the nation when 70,000 people died because "the LORD sent a plague upon Israel" (2 Samuel 24:15).

It is not wrong for you to take pride in your accomplishments, your country, or your lineage. But prideful arrogance and lording it over others with disregard for the feelings of others is sin. The Bible says pride and arrogance are two evils that God hates (Proverbs 8:13). What is the solution? Selfless and sacrificial service to others. God wants you to demonstrate this attitude: "Let nothing be done through selfish ambition or conceit, but in lowliness of mind let each esteem others better than himself. Let each of you look out not only for his own interests, but also for the interests of others" (Philippians 2:3-4).

Pride is a sin that can easily overtake us, which is why constant self-examination is so vital. The Bible gives this advice: "Examine yourselves as to whether you are in the faith. Test yourselves" (2 Corinthians 13:5).

A Man Whose Eyes Wandered

From the roof [David] saw a woman bathing,
and the woman was very beautiful to behold.

2 SAMUEL 11:2

Unfortunately, David had a problem with women. He was very human, and in today's culture he would be labeled a womanizer. David knew he had been chosen by God to be king. He also surely knew what God said in *His* law about multiplying wives. Yet he already had six wives before he married Bathsheba, and this did not include all of his concubines. David followed the example of other oriental kings by having a harem to display his wealth and power. David let his culture give him permission to fulfill his lustful passion and disregard the perfect will of God— one wife for one man.

David's unchecked passion culminated in allowing his gaze to linger long enough for lust to develop. Don't fall into the trap of thinking no one can tell what you are doing. God knows, and others can see your roving eyes, including your wife. If you are married, God has given you your own wife to love, cherish, adore, and appreciate. Every other woman is off limits and is to be treated with honor. The Bible says you are to treat "older women as mothers, younger women as sisters, with all purity" (1 Timothy 5:2). Husbands are to "rejoice with the wife of your youth" (Proverbs 5:18). God instructs, "Let your eyes look straight ahead, and your eyelids look right before you. Ponder the path of your feet, and let all your ways be established. Do not turn to the right or the left; remove your foot from evil" (Proverbs 4:25-27).

To safeguard yourself, memorize Bible verses that remind you to stay pure in thought and deed. You could start with Job 31:1: "I have made a covenant with my eyes; why then should I look upon a young woman?"

A Man Who Followed After God's Own Heart

[God] gave testimony and said,
"I have found David the son of Jesse,
a man after My own heart,
who will do all My will."

ACTS 13:22

David was among the greatest heroes of the Old Testament. He led the tiny and insignificant country of Israel to the heights of power and influence. He also established Jerusalem as the capital of the nation of Israel and brought the Ark of the Covenant to Jerusalem, establishing the city as the center of worship of the one true God. David was a great leader and his obedience to God was the key to his success.

With all that we learn about the life of David in 1 and 2 Samuel, and especially his adultery with Bathsheba and the murder of Bathsheba's husband, Uriah, it is sometimes difficult to understand how God could say that David was "a man after My own heart, who will do all My will." How was this possible? David was far from perfect, but he still loved God. When confronted with his sin, David repented, thanked God for His forgiveness, and moved on in service to God.

David's life should be a tremendous encouragement to you. Like David, you are not perfect. Just ask those closest to you! But like David, you can be a man who loves and pursues God. You grow spiritually when your greatest desire, your daily prayer, and your constant focus is to become God's kind of man. That's what it means to be a man after God's own heart. This man…

- reads and reflects on God's Word (Psalm 119:9-11).

- seeks to always obey God's Word, to be "a man who will do all His will" (Acts 13:22).

- confesses his sin quickly (1 John 1:9).

- thanks God for His amazing forgiveness in Jesus Christ (Ephesians 1:7).

A Man Who Did Not Resist Temptation

[David] saw a woman bathing, and the woman was very beautiful to behold.

2 SAMUEL 11:2

David, like his predecessor, Saul, had humble beginnings. Yet David became the greatest king in the history of Israel. He was a born leader and forged an army that made the tiny nation of Israel the most powerful Middle Eastern kingdom of his era. He established Jerusalem both as the political and religious center of the nation, and brought the ark of God to Jerusalem. He was a gifted poet, with 72 of his poems included in the book of Psalms.

Yet in spite of David's devotion to God and his excellent gifts and abilities, he failed to resist temptation and suffered greatly for sin. When David repented God forgave him, but David's family and kingdom never recovered from the consequences of his adulterous sin with Bathsheba. What life lessons can we learn from David?

No one is immune to temptation. David's fall came after

he had experienced years of immense success, which may have weakened his dependence upon God.

Never allow yourself to think you no longer need God's help with everyday living. It is in everyday living that you need God the most! Be on guard: "Sin is crouching at the door; and its desires is for you, but you must master it" (Genesis 4:7 NASB). To strengthen your relationship with God, draw near to Him through His Word, and go to Him often in prayer. A deep relationship with God takes time to build; start strengthening that relationship today.

Confession of sin is the first step to restoration. After his sin with Bathsheba, David's unrepentant heart was destroying him physically. Not until he confessed his sin—as expressed in Psalm 51—were David's heart, health, and joy restored. When you repent of sin and ask God's forgiveness, you will experience spiritual restoration and physical relief. Don't harbor sin in your life. Confess it quickly, and you will be restored.

A Man Who Had a Purpose

David, after he had served the purpose of God in his own generation, fell asleep.

ACTS 13:36 (NASB)

God had a life purpose for David, a purpose that David willingly, though faltering at times, sought and ultimately fulfilled. We could say David accomplished the will of God for his life. His heart for God guided him to be used mightily by the Lord in his own generation. He was used of God in spite of his shortcomings.

God has a life purpose for you too. Will you live out God's purpose, or your own? Wouldn't you want it to be said of you that you are serving the purpose of God? My guess is that's the desire of your heart. What man of God wouldn't want to fulfill God's grand purpose for his life? Like David, you may have stumbled and fallen into sin, but also like David, you can confess your sin and ask God to help you be more obedient day by day.

You cannot go back in time and change your past, but you can make God's purposes a reality in your life in the present—even today. How? Simply by living out God's priorities. And what are those priorities? Jesus made it simple when He said, "'You shall love the LORD your God with all your heart, with all your soul, and with all your mind.'…and…'You shall love your neighbor as yourself'" (Matthew 22:37,39). Priority one is to first love God, and priority two is to extend that love to your family and beyond.

God had a plan for David, and He has a plan for you. Starting today, you can personally and positively make a difference in the world around you. This positive effect will come naturally as you live out God's priorities, live out His Word, live close to Him through prayer, and do whatever He asks of you.

A Man Who Was a Poor Role Model

Why do...you honor your sons more than Me, to make yourselves fat with the best of all the offerings...?

1 SAMUEL 2:29

Unfortunately, the Bible does not offer very many role models for being a good dad. Much more common are negative role models like Eli. In Eli we see a case of "Like father, like sons." Eli was a priest of Israel during the last days of the judges (1 Samuel 2). For his services as a priest, he was allowed a portion of certain offerings from the people. Tragically, Eli—and his sons—abused this privilege and took more than their allotted portions.

Hear God's indictment of Eli: "Why do you kick at My sacrifice and My offering...and honor your sons more than Me, to make yourselves fat with the best of all the offerings...?" (verse 29). Did you notice the connection between father and sons? Eli was guilty of taking more of the sacrifice than he was allotted, which had made him obese. He was guilty of despising the offerings of the Lord.

And guess what? Eli's two boys were following in their dad's footsteps (verses 12-17)!

It's chilling to realize that our children are observing our lives, logging our activities, and repeating our actions, whether good or bad. Hopefully you already understand the importance of being the right kind of role model for your children. God has provided some resources to help you.

The Bible is an obvious first place to look. It presents verse after verse of the strong, consistent model of fatherhood you have in God the Father. Then there are the spiritual leaders in your local church. Learn from those who model godly parenting. Ask if any are available to mentor you. Together, these resources provide much of what you need to be a good father. The only other thing you need is desire—the desire to do whatever is needed to be God's kind of dad, a dad after God's own heart.

A Man Who Was Discouraged

[Elijah] prayed that he might die, and said…
"Now, LORD, take my life, for I am no better than
my fathers!"

1 KINGS 19:4

Elijah, a man dedicated to God, lived in a hostile society. He was bold in his confrontation surrounding the worship of the false god Baal. But he was also human and susceptible to discouragement, fear, and depression. Following his greatest victory—the execution of the 450 evil priests of Baal—Elijah was threatened by Queen Jezebel and fled into the wilderness. There, in a bout of depression, he asked God to take his life.

In response, God dealt with Elijah in a gracious way. God never rebuked the prophet. Instead, the angel of the Lord ministered to Elijah and nurtured him back to wholeness and usefulness. God knew what His servant needed—rest, food, water, and encouragement. The result? Elijah "went in the strength of that food forty days and forty nights" (1 Kings 19:8).

Elijah had his moments of despair, but he was always 100 percent devoted to God. The Lord acknowledged

Elijah's dedication, and later the prophet was honored by being taken to heaven alive in a chariot of fire (see 1 Kings 17–19; 2 Kings 1–2).

Everyone has their down times. Even with his deep commitment to God's work, Elijah still experienced times of discouragement. Because we live in a fallen world, you can be sure you will face times of fear, discouragement, and perhaps even depression. When that happens, don't lose sight of God and His ability to see you through life's trials. But you must also do your part…

- by praying. Prayer turns your focus off yourself and on to God. Prayer opens the way for God to work and changes your fears into courage and your discouragement into hope.

- by reading God's Word. The Holy Spirit uses Scripture to energize and empower you to triumph over discouragement.

- by trusting God's promises to be with you always and care for you each step of your journey.

A Man Who Was Never Alone

I have reserved seven thousand in Israel,
all whose knees have not bowed to Baal.

1 KINGS 19:18

Elijah was a prophet used mightily by God during the reigns of King Ahab and King Ahaziah. Elijah challenged the corrupt King Ahab and the priests of the false god Baal to a show of power on Mount Carmel to prove "the LORD, He is God!" (1 Kings 18:39). After God proved to be the true God and Baal to be a false god, Elijah then ordered the execution of the priests of Baal. The evil queen Jezebel, the wife of King Ahab, was enraged when she heard about the slaughter of her priests. In her desire for vengeance, she ordered the death of Elijah.

Frightened, Elijah fled to Mount Sinai. There, God revealed Himself to Elijah and commanded him to get back into the fight against false gods. Elijah thought he was alone in his defense of God's causes, but God assured Elijah that he had 7,000 others in the nation who had not bowed their knees to false gods. Even during his faltering moments, Elijah never veered from his devotion to God.

How about you? When you have your ups and downs

do you often feel as if you are alone? That no one can understand your challenges? That no one is there to help you? Like Elijah, you must remember you are not alone. And like Elijah, God will never give up on you.

Keep your eyes riveted on God through your every trial and setback, through your weariness and loneliness. Trust Him to lead and nurture you back to usefulness. Count on His promise to supply all that you need to move forward and fulfill His will. Serve the Lord gladly, faithfully, and courageously. Let Elijah's assurance from God remind you, too, that you are not alone.

A Man Who Was a Servant

[Elisha] arose and followed Elijah,
and became his servant.

1 KINGS 19:21

Elisha began his ministry as the prophet Elijah's under-study and servant. As the time approached for Elijah's departure to heaven, Elisha asked for a "double portion" of Elijah's power. Elisha was asking to succeed his mentor as a prophet with spiritual power beyond his own abilities. His request was a noble one, and God granted him 50-plus years of dynamic ministry (see 1 Kings 19:16–21; 2 Kings 2:1–13:20).

The prophetic ministry of Elisha was less spectacular than Elijah's, but it was not any less important. Elisha's ministry was to the people, not their rulers. His actions were a reflection of his gentle, loving nature, and his miracles revealed God's love, care, and concern for the needs of the less fortunate.

Elisha's life teaches us the importance of commitment. From the hour that Elijah threw his mantle over Elisha's shoulders while plowing a field, Elisha focused his life on serving God and Elijah. God might not be calling you to a high-profile public ministry, but He is asking you to be fully devoted to Him wherever you are. Remember, a commitment to God also means a commitment to God's people.

Elisha's life also teaches us that all ministry is significant. Elisha had a much less public ministry than that of Elijah, but in the economy of God, Elijah's ministry was significant in its revelation of God's love for His people. Elisha began as a simple servant, and because he was faithful, God allowed him to assume Elijah's role of God's prophet to the people. The role you play in God's plan is the role He has designed for you, and that makes you significant. Be faithful to fulfill your God-ordained role, and as you are doing your part to further God's kingdom, make sure you are passing on to others what God is teaching you—starting with your own family.

A Man Who Acted on Impulse

Esau said, "Look, I am about to die;
so what is this birthright to me?"

<small>Genesis 25:32</small>

E sau, the older twin of Jacob, was a rugged, headstrong hunter who loved being outdoors. He was the favored son of his father Isaac because of the meat Esau brought home from his hunting trips. In time, Esau became the father of the Edomites, who populated the land east of Israel. Esau and Jacob were in constant personal conflict, and later in history, their two peoples would continue their feud.

The concept of a birthright—the right of the firstborn— has been used throughout time to determine successors to kings as well as positions of authority and power in households and clans. As the older brother, Esau possessed the birthright. But foolishly, on impulse, because he was very hungry, he traded his right as the firstborn for a single bowl of stew! While explaining holiness, the author of the book of Hebrews described Esau and his conduct in this way: "Lest there be any fornicator or profane person like Esau, who for one morsel of food sold his birthright" (Hebrews

12:16). This impulsive act on Esau's part not only had physical consequences, but also spiritual implications.

Esau failed to count the cost when faced with important decisions. His choices were made according to his immediate needs rather than on their long-range impact. Unfortunately, it is all too easy for us to make fleshly decisions rather than spiritual ones—not thinking about their consequences. In Esau's case, we are told "that afterward, when [Esau] wanted to inherit the blessing, he was rejected, for he found no place for repentance, though he sought it diligently with tears" (verse 17).

The next time you are tempted to act impulsively, stop and follow this principle: No decision made without prayer. Take time to pray and think about your choices, their consequences, and how they will reflect on your Christian testimony.

A Man Who Was a Watchman

*Son of man, I have made you
a watchman for the house of Israel.*
EZEKIEL 3:17

E zekiel was part of an earlier group of Jews taken captive to Babylon. The final destruction of Jerusalem would occur eleven years later. From the beginning of his ministry, God described Ezekiel as His watchman on the wall of a city. In Ezekiel's day, a watchman had a great responsibility. He had to exercise faithful vigilance because if he failed at his post, the entire city could be destroyed. As a *spiritual* watchman, it was Ezekiel's job to faithfully warn the people of coming judgment. God commissioned Ezekiel to communicate a message of individual responsibility.

God is calling you to be one of His watchmen, a spiritual watchman. To do this, you must first watch over your own spiritual condition. Then you will be qualified to vigilantly watch and warn your family, friends, and acquaintances of the consequences of not following God's commands.

God expects personal obedience. The importance of each person's accountability before God was a central part of Ezekiel's message. Today it is easy to assume you can blend into a crowd of churchgoers and therefore not feel the weight of accountability for your actions before a holy God. But when you read Ezekiel's warnings to the people of Judah, you will realize that God is personally interested in you and your actions. In light of this, are there any changes you need to make in the way you live? Don't delay. Be quick to make things right with God so you can fulfill your role as a spiritual watchman.

God always gives hope, even in the darkest hour. In Judah's darkest hour, Ezekiel brought God's message of bright hope for the future. Today you may be experiencing bleak and dark circumstances, but don't despair. There is help when you draw on Jesus's strength and power. Remember, if you have the light of Jesus in your life, you will never be alone when you face a dark hour.

A Man Whose Authority Was God's Word

Ezra had prepared his heart
to seek the Law of the LORD, and to do it.
EZRA 7:1

E zra was a priest living in exile in the land of Persia. Long before the Persian king commissioned Ezra to lead a group of Jews back to Jerusalem, God was preparing Ezra for this assignment. Don't fail to note Ezra's heart not only for God, but for His Word.

- First, as a scribe, Ezra devoted himself to the careful study of God's Word.

- Second, Ezra determined to personally apply and obey what he was learning from Scripture.

- Third, Ezra desired to teach others to know and obey God's Word (Ezra 7:10).

It's no surprise that Ezra had such a major impact on people as he kept these priorities:

He understood the importance of God's Word. Three steps—study, apply, and obey God's Word—are essential to your spiritual growth. Ezra's achievements can be directly attributed to his commitment to living his life by the standards in God's Word. As you do the same, you will achieve growth in your relationship with God.

He trusted God with all aspects of his life. Ezra could have chosen not to take any chances on what he knew would be a difficult task and journey (Ezra 7:1-8). Instead, he relied on the power of God to provide and care for him. Ezra trusted God, and so should you. What areas of your life need to be committed into the all-powerful hands of God?

Hold fast to the authority of Scripture. Ezra was unwilling to compromise the truths taught in God's Word. To Ezra, the Scriptures were not open for reinterpretation. God's written Word is perfectly clear. Accept its authority in your life, and model its authority to others. Your life is the only Bible some people may ever read. Your example may speak more loudly to some people than your teaching. As the saying goes, "Don't just talk the talk; also walk the walk."

A Man Who Asked for a Sign

If now I have found favor in Your sight,
then show me a sign.

JUDGES 6:17

Gideon was a judge in Israel during a time when the nation was under the oppression of the Midianites. This had come about because of Israel's disobedience against God. The Lord called Gideon to destroy not only an altar built in tribute to a false god called Baal, but also to defeat the massive Midianite army. Because Gideon had weak faith, he requested two signs—a wet fleece and then a dry fleece—so he could know whether or not God truly would use a simple farmer like him to save Israel. God gave Gideon the signs that affirmed he would know victory, but to ensure that the people would know that the victory came from the Lord Himself, God commanded that Gideon's army of 22,000 men be reduced to 300 men.

Armed only with trumpets and torches hidden in clay pitchers, Gideon's small force prevailed. Later Gideon refused the people's offer to make him their king, saying that neither he nor his son would rule over the people, but the Lord God would.

Are you asking God for a sign? Gideon wanted proof that he, a simple farmer, could truly defeat the powerful Midianite army. Graciously, God gave him a sign—actually, two signs. More importantly, God gave him a dramatic victory. Now, how about you? Most of us like to think that if we were visited by God we would never question God and ask for proof. But think about this: Every time you open God's Word and fail to respond in faith to His message, you are following in Gideon's steps. If you want to have more of God's guidance, don't "put out a fleece." Ask for faith to believe, and trust that God will follow through: "Now faith is the assurance of things hoped for, the conviction of things not seen" (Hebrews 11:1 NASB).

A Man Who Relied on Physical Strength

A champion went out from the camp of the Philistines, named Goliath.

1 SAMUEL 17:4

Have you ever stood next to an NFL or NBA player? These athletes are incredibly large and imposing. Now imagine standing before a man who stood more than nine feet tall. That would be intimidating! Goliath was a giant with no lack of self-confidence, and his mere presence immobilized the entire army of Israel. Brandishing his massive armor and weapons, he blasphemed Israel's God and challenged one of Israel's men to duel with him. Goliath had no doubt that he could defeat anyone with his might and power.

It never occurred to Goliath that he was vulnerable until a young boy named David threw a small stone that lodged between Goliath's eyes. Prior to the showdown, David had been offered King Saul's armor, but it didn't fit. David then turned to the two weapons he knew he could rely on—his trust in God and his shepherd's sling.

Too often we enter into our daily battles thinking like

Goliath did. We don't necessarily count on our physical size and strength, but we let our pride and ego make us think we can defeat the world. Like Goliath, we don't recognize our vulnerabilities. The apostle Paul gave the right perspective when he said, "The weapons we fight with are not the weapons of the world. On the contrary, they have divine power to demolish strongholds" (2 Corinthians 10:4 NIV).

Don't face the world on its terms or try to match its weapons. Instead, accept the resources that God offers in Ephesians 6:10-18: "Put on the whole armor of God, that you may be able to stand against the wiles of the devil" (verse 11). God's armor and weapons are not of this world, and therefore they will never fail. How much of God's spiritual armor are you wearing today? Armor up and fight the good fight of faith!

A Man Who Made a Difference

[Hezekiah] did what was right in the sight of the LORD, according to all that his father David had done.

2 KINGS 18:3

Hezekiah, whose name means "strength of Yahweh" or "strength of God," was one of the kings of the southern kingdom of Judah. Unlike his predecessor, Hezekiah was a righteous king. In 2 Kings 18:5 he was commended for his faithfulness to God. Hezekiah was perhaps best known for his prayer life. In one prayer, Hezekiah asked God to intervene against the invading Assyrian army. God answered by killing 185,000 men in the Assyrian camp, causing the Assyrian King Sennacherib to flee. In another prayer, Hezekiah asked God to intervene in his terminal illness. God answered and granted Hezekiah an additional 15 years of life.

Like Hezekiah, you can make a difference! You don't have to wonder if heredity or environment shapes your destiny. Hezekiah defied both. His earthly father, Ahaz, was an idolater who closed the temple and set up idols for pagan worship throughout the land. In sharp contrast,

Hezekiah brought about a major spiritual reformation and pointed the people back to God. He was one of very few kings in Judah's history whom God compared favorably with his ancestor, King David.

You might be asking, "But how can I make a difference? I'm just one insignificant person!" Well, you can thank God that He has given you two incredible weapons so you can have an impact!

Weapon 1: Like Hezekiah, you have the weapon of prayer. We are told in the New Testament that prayer makes a difference: "The effective, fervent prayer of a righteous man avails much" (James 5:16).

Weapon 2: Like Hezekiah, you can use character as a powerful weapon—you can be "a righteous man."

Your prayer life and your godly character will shine light into a dark world.

A Man Who Had a Quiet Spirit

[Isaac] said, "She is my sister"; for he was afraid to say, "She is my wife."

GENESIS 26:7

I saac is significant because he was a transitional figure: The promise made by God to *Abraham* that God would make Abraham a great nation was passed down to *Isaac*, who would later pass that inheritance down to his son, *Jacob*. Isaac's quiet spirit served him well when early in his life, by faith and in trust in God, he offered no objection when his father, Abraham, obeyed God by raising a knife to slay him (Genesis 22:1-10).

Isaac later married Rebekah, and they had twin sons, Esau and Jacob. The low point in their marriage came when, like his father Abraham, Isaac asked his wife, Rebekah, to lie about their marital relationship. When his cowardly lie was discovered, the king of the Philistines confronted him (Genesis 26:6-9). Isaac's quiet spirit was again seen in his refusal to be provoked when his enemies claimed his water wells as their own (Genesis 26:15-21).

Isaac was content to live quietly in the Promised Land, tending to his flocks and herds. In Matthew 5:9, Jesus spoke of the blessings of being a peacemaker. But Isaac's passive nature had its dark side, which became evident when he refused to defend and protect his wife against the possibility of sexual defilement. A quiet nature is a good asset to have in our violent world, but it is never to be used at the expense of your character, responsibilities, or obedience to God's standards. Trust God to help you as you stand up for what you know is right. God will protect and honor your courage. In addition, having a quiet spirit is not a license or excuse for inactivity. Never settle for the status quo. A quiet spirit can actively move forward with boldness in the course of serving God.

A Man Who Had a Favorite Son

Isaac loved Esau because he ate of his game.
GENESIS 25:28

Isaac was the promised and long-awaited son of Abraham and Sarah. He married Rebekah, who came from his father's homeland in Mesopotamia, and they had twin sons, Esau and Jacob. Unfortunately, each parent had a favorite son. Isaac loved Esau for his rough and rugged manner and his hunting skills. Rebekah loved Jacob for his mildness and his desire to be a homebody. With his mother's help, Jacob deceived his father into giving him "the blessing" that should have gone to the eldest son, which was Esau. This deception and a lifetime of favoritism forced Isaac to send Jacob to Rebekah's family to protect him against Esau's vow of vengeance over the stolen blessing. The parents' favoritism led to the permanent dissolution of Isaac's family.

As we can see from Isaac's home, favoritism leads to strife and division. If you are a parent, avoid the temptation to treat any of your children as a "little you," expecting that child to follow in your steps or pursue your goals and ambitions. Each of your children is a unique gift from

God. Each child has been fashioned by the hand of God, and it is much better to praise the unique qualities and abilities of each of your children rather than favor the one child whose strengths or personality you like most.

It is also important to guard against favoritism in your church family: "My brethren, do not hold your faith in our glorious Lord Jesus Christ with an attitude of personal favoritism" (James 2:1 NASB). James condemned treating one class of people better than another based on their clothing (verses 2-7). If you say that Christ is your Lord, then you must live as He requires, showing no favoritism and loving all people, regardless of whether they are rich or poor.

A Man Who Had a Willing Heart

I heard the voice of the Lord, saying:
"Whom shall I send…?"
Then I said, "Here am I! Send me."
ISAIAH 6:8

Isaiah was a prophet who volunteered to take God's message to the people in and around Jerusalem. His ministry spanned 53 years, through the reigns of four kings. Isaiah condemned the empty ritualism of his day and the people's idolatry. He predicted the coming Babylonian captivity of Judah because of their sin. More than any other prophet, Isaiah furnished data on the coming day of the Lord and Israel's future kingdom on earth. God used Isaiah to prophesy many events, including the birth of Jesus, the Messiah, and His death on behalf of mankind. What are some truths we learn from the life of Isaiah?

Service to God doesn't require public notice. Isaiah was a great man with a prominent ministry, yet little is known of his life. His motivation for ministry was not driven by a need for public distinction or to be the center of attention. He wanted only to do his part. Can you do your part and say, "Here am I! Send me"? Seek to serve God and

His people without desiring the public spotlight. Service to God in any capacity is reward enough.

A righteous God requires a righteous response. Isaiah's vision of the holiness of God made him humbly aware of the judgment he deserved for his own sinful condition. Like Isaiah, live your life in light of God's holiness. A sense of unworthiness followed by thankfulness should be your response every time you come into the presence of God through prayer.

God's message must be faithfully communicated in spite of the response. Isaiah eagerly responded to God's call and faithfully proclaimed God's message for more than 50 years. Even though kings and others ignored his warnings, he kept preaching anyway. God is asking you, too, to faithfully communicate the message of Jesus Christ, and to leave the response in His hands.

A Man Who Was a Victim

Drive out this maid and her son
for the son of this maid
shall not be an heir with my son Isaac.

GENESIS 21:10 (NASB)

Why do bad things happen to good people? Why are innocent people involved in tragedies? So many things happen that don't make sense and don't seem to be fair. Ishmael might have been mulling over these same questions as he and his mother, Hagar, were sent away from their home through no fault of their own. Until this took place, Ishmael had been treated as a son and heir in his father Abraham's house. Suddenly he was a homeless person with no hope for the future—or at least it looked that way. He was a victim...or was he?

God did not abandon this teenager. God had told Abraham, before he sent Ishmael away, "I will also make a nation of the son of the bondwoman, because he is your seed" (Genesis 21:13). And sure enough, in God's timing, Ishmael had many descendants and became the father of many nations. God's provision and protection of Ishmael is a testimony to God's faithfulness and His sovereign plan.

There are no "victims" in God's plans for His people—including you—as Romans 8:28 affirms: "We know that all things work together for good to those who love God, to those who are the called according to His purpose." God orchestrates every aspect of your life to accomplish His purposes. You are not a victim of what has happened in your past, or what is now happening or will happen in the future. There are no mistakes with God. Every event and every so-called "tragedy" is happening for your good and God's glory.

You might not think so today, but every trial you undergo is an opportunity for God to strengthen your spiritual muscles. An opportunity for you to experience God's divine grace one more time. An opportunity to experience God's promise, "My grace is sufficient for you, for My strength is made perfect in weakness" (2 Corinthians 12:9).

A Man Who Was Selfish

Jacob said to his household…
"Put away the foreign gods that are among you."
GENESIS 35:2

Jacob was plain old selfish! It's hard to gloss over this character flaw and these facts about Jacob.

- He wanted Esau's birthright, and took it.

- He wanted his father's blessing, and allowed his willing mother to help him deceive his father.

- He wanted Rachel as his wife and didn't care who he hurt while pursuing her.

- He wanted wealth and showed little interest in his family.

Do we need to go on? The tragedy is that Jacob got everything he went after, but lost his family in the process. For Jacob, God, marriage, and family didn't seem to be priorities. Jacob evidently was so preoccupied with himself and his problems with his father-in-law that he forgot to educate his family in the ways of God until it was too late. As a result, his family embraced foreign gods. This pagan influence would follow Jacob's family for centuries, and eventually they were carried away into captivity because of their idolatry.

Like Jacob, you live in a pagan society. What are you doing to insulate your faith in Christ and ensure that it is passed on to your family? Are you so busy doing your own thing that you aren't providing strong spiritual direction for your family? You don't have to be a Bible school student to be the spiritual leader of your family. If you feel inadequate, seek help from leaders in your church. The spiritual leadership you provide for your family can be as simple as reading from the Bible together as a family. Do what God expects of you, and live out your faith. Take some time each day to share spiritual things with those at home. It's easy to be selfish or think you are too busy, but leading, loving, and teaching your family will yield incredible rewards and eternal results.

A Man Who Lived by Deception

[Isaac] said, "Are you really my son Esau?"
He [Jacob] said, "I am."

GENESIS 27:24

Jacob (whose name means "trickster," "heel-grabber," or "supplanter") was a twin boy born to Isaac and Rebekah, and he definitely lived up to his name! In his early life Jacob had a pronounced tendency to lie, deceive, manipulate, and take matters into his own hands. And Jacob's mother, Rebakah, didn't help. She encouraged Jacob to deceive his father, Isaac, and receive the blessing meant for the elder son, Esau. There are always consequences to sin. In the end, Jacob had to flee for his life and never again saw his mother alive.

After Jacob fled from his childhood home, he himself was lied to and deceived by others, including his conniving father-in-law, Laban. This led him to begin looking to God for guidance. By the end of his life, Jacob was far more reliant upon asking for God's direction rather than doing things his own way.

The end never justifies the manipulation of our circumstances, and especially if we resort to deception. God condemns deception and blesses truthfulness: "Lying lips are an abomination to the LORD, but those who deal truthfully are His delight" (Proverbs 12:22).

Rather than seeking to deceive your way out of a situation as Jacob did, view your circumstances as an opportunity to trust God and grow spiritually. God wants you to learn from your problems, not avoid or resent them. Embrace your life as it is with all its trials. Ask God to strengthen you and give you a more trusting heart. As Jacob finally realized, you can experience God's solutions, which are always the best ones! God does not need your help to accomplish His will, so trust Him to work out your circumstances.

A Man Who Cried Out to God

*They surrounded him to attack; but Jehoshaphat
cried out, and the LORD helped him.*

2 CHRONICLES 18:31

Jehoshaphat was one of the good kings of the southern kingdom. First Kings 22:43 tells us, "He did not turn aside from…doing what was right in the eyes of the LORD." Unfortunately, Jehoshaphat made his share of mistakes. First, he allowed his son to marry Athaliah, the daughter of Ahab and Jezebel. Then, without asking God, he made an alliance with Ahab, who persuaded Jehoshaphat to join forces and attack a common enemy. God warned Jehoshaphat through the prophet Micaiah that their plans would not succeed, but Jehoshaphat ignored the warning and proceeded into battle, demonstrating willful disobedience.

Almost immediately, Jehoshaphat was in trouble and he knew it. The opposing army mistook him for King Ahab, and Jehoshaphat became the focused target of their attack. At that moment he could accept his fate, knowing he was guilty before God, and try to fight his way out of the impossible situation. Or he could swallow his pride and cry out to God for deliverance. He chose wisely—to cry out to God—and God miraculously saved him.

Admitting you are wrong is hard. What's even harder is admitting you have sinned. Instead of pointing you to God for His forgiveness and restoration, pride propels you in the opposite direction, away from God. That's what Adam and Eve did in the Garden of Eden. They hid from God. King David also refused to go to God when he committed adultery with Bathsheba. The consequence? David admitted, "When I kept silent, my bones grew old through my groaning all the day long...My vitality was turned into the drought of summer" (Psalm 32:3-4).

If you are harboring unconfessed sin and are trying to run from God, stop. Jehoshaphat's plight shows us that turning to God—crying out to Him—is always the right course of action. No matter how great or small your sin, God is willing to graciously forgive you.

A Man Who Stayed on Task

You will keep him in perfect peace,
whose mind is stayed on You,
because he trusts in You.

ISAIAH 26:3

Sometimes it's hard to stay focused, to stay on task, especially if your direction is unpopular! Jeremiah, however, was able to persevere, even while he faced intense persecution and ridicule. Jeremiah faithfully communicated God's word to His people for 40 years, warning them about the doom and captivity that was sure to come unless they repented and turned to God. But no one listened to Jeremiah.

Jeremiah often lost hope regarding the job God gave him as a prophet. Even the people in Jeremiah's own city hated him. His messages were definitely not popular. But Jeremiah remained obedient to his calling to warn the people. Even in his despair, he praised God.

Even though he suffered immensely for it, Jeremiah was faithful to God. Against all odds, he stayed on task, preaching and warning God's people. What was the cost of such commitment? People hated and threatened Jeremiah, and even whipped and imprisoned him. Yet Jeremiah refused to waver from God's assignment. He endured in spite of difficulties. He preached on…and on…for 40 years, even with no response. Yet God continually encouraged Jeremiah.

You may never face the level of persecution experienced by Jeremiah, but wherever life finds you, you can still draw on the same resources and encouragement God made available to Jeremiah. In whatever situation you are facing, don't balk, fall back, drop out, or quit. Stay the course. In spite of any persecution or scorn, turn to God. Review and renew your commitment to Him. Count on His grace to see you through any and all problems. Like Jeremiah, keep your heart and mind fixed on Him and do as he did—"Praise the LORD!" (Jeremiah 20:13).

A Man Who Had Secondhand Faith

Joash did what was right in the sight of the LORD all the days of Jehoiada the priest.

2 CHRONICLES 24:2

Being a leader of any kind is difficult at any age, but especially if you are only seven years old! Tragedy had struck the kingdom of Judah with the death of King Ahaziah (2 Kings 9:27) and the subsequent murders of all the king's sons, except one, Joash. What made the killings even more horrific was that they were carried out by Athaliah, Joash's grandmother. Joash was kept hidden for six years before Athaliah was killed, and then he became the boy-king (2 Kings 11).

Initially, Joash listened to the godly advice of a priest named Jehoiada, and he made many improvements on the temple and made sure that sacrifices and burnt offerings were faithfully made to the God of Israel. But after Jehoiada died, Joash almost immediately abandoned his godly pursuits. When Jehoiada's son, Zechariah, rebuked the king, Joash ordered his execution, and it wasn't long before Joash was assassinated.

Joash is a prime example of secondhand faith. His earlier decisions were not based on a heart of true belief, but on the faith of another—Jehoiada. When Jehoiada was alive, Joash acted like a true believer. But when Jehoiada's godly influence was gone, Joash's true unbelieving nature became evident.

It's easy to "play church" when you are at church or around Christians, but what about the rest of the week? Does your commitment change with your circumstance? One of the true tests of whether your faith is real is how you act around unbelievers. If you are struggling to maintain a Christian witness in a hostile and unbelieving world, read the first six chapters of the book of Daniel. Daniel lived his life under pagan influences, yet his enemies admitted that he passed the true faith test: "We shall not find any charge against this Daniel unless we find it against him concerning the law of his God" (Daniel 6:5).

What is the world saying about you and your faith?

A Man Who Suffered for the Glory of God

*Through all this Job did not sin
nor did he blame God.*

JOB 1:22 (NASB)

Job lived around the same time as Abraham, the father of the Hebrew nation. Job was a wealthy, influential leader and a loving husband and father. One day, within the span of a few hours, he lost everything through a series of disasters. Job was left with nothing but his faith in God and questions as to why these calamities had happened to him.

Job never learned why God had permitted him to suffer, but he did learn to accept his situation without questioning God's character, wisdom, and judgment. The Job who persevered through his suffering knew God better and trusted Him more deeply than the Job who entered those trials.

What can you learn from Job?

Suffering should be viewed from a divine perspective. Like Job in his early days, you may be living a trouble-free life. Yet God never promised life will always be carefree.

Suffering will come, and we are to learn to view it from a divine perspective. When you suffer, God is working in ways that you often will not or cannot understand. These perplexing times are opportunities to strengthen your faith in the wisdom of God and increase your confidence in His grace to see you through: "My grace is sufficient for you, for My strength is made perfect in weakness" (2 Corinthians 12:9).

Suffering should be for the glory of God. When hard times show up on your doorstep, stay faithful to God. Continue to love Him and serve Him, to trust Him and look to Him. Like Job, be unwavering in your walk with God. Do what is right. Praise God with your lips. Humble yourself before Him. Believe that He is in constant control… no matter what. As you remain faithful in your suffering, God is honored and glorified.

A Man Who Was Given a Second Opportunity

When my soul fainted within me,
I remembered the LORD.

JONAH 2:7

Jonah was a reluctant prophet who did not want to fulfill his God-commanded mission to preach a message of judgment to the dreaded Assyrians at Nineveh. His contempt for the Ninevites was so strong that he chose to run away from God rather than obey Him. After being miraculously swallowed by a large fish, Jonah came to his senses (Jonah 2).

God overlooked Jonah's rebellion and gave him a second chance to serve Him. God once again commanded him to travel to Nineveh to preach God's message. And sure enough, Jonah's worst fear came true: Most of the people in the city repented! Jonah was extremely angry that God had decided to spare Nineveh. Jonah was more concerned about his national pride than about people who were spiritually lost, especially because they were his nation's enemy. Yet through all of this, God never gave up on Jonah.

God was gracious to both the people of Nineveh and Jonah. Maybe you feel as though God has given up on you, or you believe your sin and failure are too much for God to forgive. But God's patience and kindness is available to you as well. King David knew about second chances; he wrote, "I acknowledged my sin to You, and my iniquity I have not hidden. I said, 'I will confess my transgressions to the LORD,' and You forgave the iniquity of my sin" (Psalm 32:5).

God is ready to give you a second chance, but you must do your part. Cease running away from Him and turn to Him in repentance. Ask for His forgiveness. Then you too can shout along with David, "Blessed is he whose transgression is forgiven, whose sin is covered!" (Psalm 32:1). What a gracious God you have!

A Man Who Was a Loyal Friend

*Jonathan…went to David in the woods
and strengthened his hand in God.*

1 SAMUEL 23:16

Surely you have had experience with a "fair-weather friend." This person sticks around as long as things go well. Usually such a friendship is a one-way street. As long as the other person is happy, everything is fine. But the minute you disagree or a problem comes along, that "friend" fades away in the night, wanting nothing to do with you. By contrast, a true friend is loyal.

The friendship between Jonathan and David as described in the Bible was characterized by fierce loyalty even in the midst of adversity. When David was marked for murder by Jonathan's father, King Saul, "Jonathan went to David… and helped him find strength in God" (1 Samuel 23:16 NIV). It's surprising that Jonathan would still want to be David's friend because…

- God had selected David instead of Jonathan to be the next king.

- Jonathan's father was insanely jealous of David and tried to kill him repeatedly.

- David was extremely talented and much more popular with the people than either Jonathan or his father.

For these reasons, Jonathan could have rejected David. Instead, he remained David's most loyal and trusted friend and a source of encouragement in the Lord.

How loyal are you as a friend? Are you "a friend who sticks closer than a brother" (Proverbs 18:24)? The loyalty of others starts with you being loyal to them. The best way to be loyal to your friends is to hold them to a high standard—God's standard. Your role is not to tell them what you think they *want* to hear, but what they *need* to hear. Your first priority is to help them "find strength in God" through the Scriptures and through praying together. This is what it means to be a loyal friend.

A Man Who Had a God-Perspective

You meant evil against me;
but God meant it for good.

GENESIS 50:20

Joseph was the eleventh of the twelve sons of Jacob. He was born of Rachel, the wife Jacob loved most. It's no wonder, then, that Joseph was Jacob's favorite son. This made Joseph's brothers jealous. Things were made worse by Joseph's dreams depicting his brothers bowing down before him. As a result, Joseph's brothers resented him deeply, and when an opportunity arose to get rid of him, they did. They sold Joseph as a slave to merchants traveling to Egypt.

Joseph suffered unjustly, but he steadfastly trusted God, consistently made right choices, and ultimately was exalted to second in command over all of Egypt. In spite of the many injustices he faced because of the wrong done to him by his brothers, Joseph showed tremendous grace by forgiving them and welcoming them to share God's blessings with him in the land of Egypt. Joseph looked beyond his brothers' deeds, knowing that God was in control. As he explained to his family, "You meant evil against me; but God meant it for good, in order to bring it about as it is this day, to save many people alive" (Genesis 50:20).

Do you believe that God always has your best interest at heart? Maybe you are going through a rough time today, and you can't see how anything good could come from your present circumstance. It is during times of trial that you must look beyond your present state of affairs and trust God, believing He is working out His will for you. To have Joseph's God-perspective, do and believe as the apostle Paul wrote: "We know that all things work together for good to those who love God, to those who are the called according to His purpose" (Romans 8:28). No matter what happens, always trust God. Believe He is working for your good and His glory.

A Man Who Chose Not to Sin

How then can I do this great wickedness,
and sin against God?

GENESIS 39:9

Rachel was Jacob's favorite wife, which made Joseph, Rachel's son, special in his father's eyes. However, because of Jacob's favoritism and Joseph's inability to keep his prophetic dreams to himself, Joseph was sold into slavery in Egypt by his brothers. Joseph could have become bitter and rebellious toward God. And when the opportunity came to have a secret sexual affair with his master's wife, Joseph could have thought, *Why not abandon God, since He seems to have abandoned me?*

But Joseph's response was just the opposite. He said, "How then can I do this great wickedness, and sin against God?" (Genesis 39:9). He understood that sin not only has physical consequences, but spiritual consequences as well. Joseph's response to the adversities and temptations he faced revealed the true state of his heart. Joseph was a man of impeccable character and integrity—a man who refused to participate in sin.

What's in your heart? Do you blame God when adversity

comes along? Do you turn your back on God and His commands in Scripture? Do you rationalize wrong behavior when temptation comes your way? Don't let problems pull you down. These are the encouraging words Jesus gave to His disciples before He went to the cross: "In the world you will have tribulation; but be of good cheer, I have overcome the world" (John 16:33).

God did not abandon Joseph, and He will not abandon you. You are not alone as you face sin and temptation. Remember, Jesus has already made victory possible for you. Temptations and the opportunities to sin will always abound. But you can overcome them, because the victory has already been won and secured by Jesus.

A Man Who Was Successful

*Then you will make your way prosperous,
and then you will have good success.*

JOSHUA 1:8

When Moses died, Joshua became the new leader of the nation of Israel. Before his death, Moses passed the baton of leadership to Joshua. This had to be a frightening position for Joshua to take on. Moses, the great leader who had guided two million people out of Egypt, through the desert, and to the border of a new land, had chosen Joshua to take command!

God knew Joshua was fearful—and twice in Joshua chapter 1, God told him to be strong and courageous (verses 7,9). God also gave Joshua a strategy for success. And please note: God's formula for success goes against everything the world would suggest. According to Joshua 1:8, to be successful, Joshua would need to...

- study God's Word constantly—"This Book of the Law shall not depart from your mouth."

- ponder God's Word continually—"You shall meditate in it day and night."

- apply God's Word completely—"That you may observe to do according to all that is written in it."

Joshua followed God's advice, and God gave him success. Joshua conquered the land and divided it among the 12 tribes. He prospered in his personal life, and he served as a good spiritual example his entire life.

This is the same strategy you can follow for success—not according to the world's standards, but according to God's. God's success begins with God's Word—reading it, studying it, memorizing it, thinking on it, loving it, knowing you need it, and obeying it. As you are faithful, God will fulfill His promise: "You will have success"—His kind of success.

Isn't this the ultimate definition of success, living your life according to God's will, in a way that pleases Him with your every action and attitude?

A Man Who Went the Distance

As for me and my house,
we will serve the LORD.

JOSHUA 24:15

J oshua (whose name means "Yahweh is salvation") is
first mentioned in Exodus 17:9, where Joshua received
orders from Moses to organize an army against the dreaded
Amalekites. Joshua was Moses's servant and assistant for
40 years. He was also one of the 12 spies Moses sent into
the Promised Land to gather vital information about the
land and its people. Only Joshua and Caleb brought back a
positive report. Therefore, they were the only ones of their
generation permitted to later enter the land of Canaan
because of their trust in God to give them victory over
the Canaanites.

After Moses died, Joshua led the people of Israel on military campaigns throughout Canaan, eventually conquering
the entire land and dividing it up among the people. Joshua
was committed to obeying God fully, and he was devoted
to ensuring that the people followed God all the days of
his life. When their faithfulness faltered, Joshua gave a
challenge to the people to follow his example, declaring,

"As for me and my house, we will serve the LORD" (Joshua 24:15). Not one negative word is recorded in the Bible about Joshua, the servant of both God and Moses.

How would others rate your faithfulness to your earthly leaders and your heavenly Father? Commitment is not a sprint; it is a lifelong marathon! Ask God to give you the desire to go the distance in your commitments to your family, your church, your work, and especially your Lord.

A Man Who Responded to God's Word

When the king heard the words of the law, he tore his clothes.

2 CHRONICLES 34:19 (NASB)

Josiah had the notable distinction of being the king that led the last great religious revival in Judah. Josiah was only eight years old when he became king. Unfortunately, he was destined to follow in the wicked footsteps of both his grandfather and his father, and he continued the evil practices of these two men.

However, at the age of 16, Josiah made a dramatic change—"He began to seek the God of his father David" (2 Chronicles 34:3). As a result, Josiah made efforts to purge the land of idolatry. While repairs were being made on the temple, a copy of the law was found in the rubble and Josiah had it read to him. His response was immediate! "When the king heard the words of the law, he tore his clothes" to express his deep grief and remorse. Josiah was shocked when he realized how far the nation had strayed from God's laws.

Josiah did not experience a mere moment of remorse

and then let his passion die. No, he immediately began making radical decisions about how to comply with what God expected of him and his people (2 Kings 23).

When you hear God's Word preached or when you read the Scriptures for yourself, are you momentarily moved, only to later return to your lukewarm ways or attitudes? Are you numb to what you are hearing or reading? God has given you His Word to change your life! In the Bible, God gives "to us all things that pertain to life and godliness, through the knowledge of Him" (2 Peter 1:3). When it comes to God's Word, don't delay or procrastinate. Josiah gives you the right response. Determine today that with God's help you will listen, read, respond, and obey completely as He speaks to you through His Word.

A Man Who Had a Change of Heart

The scepter shall not depart from Judah,
nor a lawgiver from between his feet.

GENESIS 49:10

In his earlier years, Judah was opportunistic, selfish, dishonest, and indifferent to the sufferings of others. We are first exposed to Judah's lack of character when he urges his brothers to sell their young brother, Joseph, into slavery rather than kill him. Judah's actions toward Joseph were less than honorable. In his scheming heart, he thought, *Why not make a little money off of this trouble-some and arrogant brother?* For a long time, Judah's character did not improve. For example, he lied to Tamar, his daughter-in-law, and failed to keep a promise he made to her, acting hypocritically in the process (Genesis 37–38).

Later in his life, we see a different Judah. When his youngest brother Benjamin was arrested and falsely accused of theft, Judah pleaded, "Please let [me] your servant remain instead of the lad as a slave to my lord" (Genesis 44:33-34). The boy was released, and Judah went on to become the leader of his tribe. Even though he wasn't the firstborn, Judah "prevailed over his brothers and from him came a ruler" (1 Chronicles 5:2). These words were a prophecy of the coming of David and ultimately the Lord Jesus Christ.

Judah's transformation can serve as a reminder of the promise in 2 Corinthians 5:17: "If anyone is in Christ, he is a new creation; old things have passed away; behold, all things have become new." If you are a new creation, how's your transformation coming along? Are there areas of your life that you are holding back from God? If so, give them over to Him, and move on to the next level of character development.

A Checklist for Character

Do you keep your promises?

Do you check for wrong motives before you act?

Do you deal favorably with your family members?

Do you allow money to influence your decisions?

A Man Who Was Worldly

Lot lifted his eyes
and saw all the plain of Jordan,
that it was well watered.

GENESIS 13:10

After the death of his father, Abraham took Sarah, his wife, and his nephew, Lot, and followed God's directive to go to a new land—to Canaan. As time passed, God blessed both men so abundantly that their flocks and herds grew to the point that the land could not sustain them both. As a result, Abraham took his nephew to a high hill and asked him to choose between the lush valley below or the rocky hill country. Lot saw what he wanted to see, the land that "was well watered," and made his choice, and Abraham accepted the hill country. Lot made his choice based on what the Bible describes as "the lust of the flesh, the lust of the eyes, and the pride of life," which "is not of the Father but is of the world" (1 John 2:16).

Lot was not bothered by the fact that he pitched his tent near Sodom and that "the men of Sodom were exceedingly wicked and sinful against the LORD" (Genesis 13:13). He didn't seem too concerned about the consequences that might come with this choice. And He never consulted with God. Lot only saw life through the lustful eyes of the world. What was the aftermath of his choice? Lot lost everything, including his possessions, his wife, and his daughters, who were so influenced by the corrupt society that they made many immoral decisions (Genesis 19).

Don't be fooled into looking at life through the world's eyes. Scripture warns, "Do not love the world or the things in the world. If anyone loves the world, the love of the Father is not in him" (1 John 2:15). Instead, "set your mind on things above, not on things on the earth" (Colossians 3:2). Which will you choose: the *world*, which is passing away, or *heaven*, which is forever? Doesn't seem like such a difficult choice, does it?

A Man Who Worked for the Good of Others

Mordecai the Jew…
was great among the Jews…
seeking the good of his people.

ESTHER 10:3

Mordecai was a Jew who lived in Persia around 540 BC. He must have served in a position of prominence because he spent his time "within the king's gate," a place where disputes were heard and verdicts were rendered (Esther 2:21). On one occasion Mordecai overheard a plot to kill the king. He passed this information on to his cousin, Esther, who had become queen, and the assassination attempt was foiled. Later, when the evil Haman was exposed and executed for wanting to exterminate the Jews in all of Persia, Mordecai became prime minister in his place. The Bible records that Mordecai "was great among the Jews and well received by the multitude of his brethren, seeking the good of his people and speaking peace to all his countrymen" (Esther 10:3).

This same praise was given of Jesus while He was on earth: He "went about doing good" (Acts 10:38). With all the evil that is around us, wouldn't it be admirable to be known as a man who works for the good of others? The fruit of the Spirit includes "goodness" (Galatians 5:22-23). As you are obedient to God and controlled by His Spirit, you can be a person filled with goodness.

To get started,

- approach each day with a desire to make a positive difference in the lives of the people God places in your path.

- follow Paul's advice to "not grow weary while doing good" (Galatians 6:9).

Why not start today? A phone call can do a lot of good for someone who is hurting. And texting or emailing a Scripture passage can bolster the spirit of one who is discouraged. Like Mordecai, use your status, your resources, and your influence to work for the good of others.

A Man Who Had an Anger Problem

"Hear now, you rebels!
Must we bring water for you out of this rock?"
Then Moses lifted his hand
and struck the rock twice with his rod.

NUMBERS 20:11

Moses was chosen by God to lead the people of Israel out of the land of Egypt and into the Promised Land. With the help of his brother, Aaron, Moses confronted Pharaoh, who was oppressing the children of Israel as slaves. God hardened Pharaoh's heart and sent ten plagues upon Egypt before Pharaoh finally let God's people go, and Moses triumphantly led the Israelites out of Egypt.

As God's people approached the Promised Land, they failed to trust Him and were afraid of the size of the people in the land. God then punished the Israelites and condemned them to wander in the wilderness for 40 years.

As with all men, Moses was far from perfect. Unfortunately, it was during those less-than-perfect times that his anger got the best of him and his life was altered forever. In anger he killed an Egyptian who was harming an Israelite slave

(Exodus 2:12), and as a result had to flee for his life. Later, after 40 years of dealing with the contention, complaints, and disobedience of the people, Moses's anger clouded his judgment once again. Rather than speak to the rock as directed by God so the people could have water, Moses struck the rock in anger—twice. His anger cost him permission to enter into the Promised Land.

The Bible tells us that it is important to handle our anger properly, to not let it linger so that Satan can use it to cause us to sin (Ephesians 4:26). Unfortunately, most of our anger is not righteous anger, but the result of pride and selfishness. We don't get what we want, so we get mad, and this outburst is expressed in harmful and disruptive ways. Anger is a quick, easy, and explosive emotion Satan can use to destroy your Christian testimony. The next time your anger seems to be getting the best of you, remember Moses and the disastrous consequences of his actions.

A Man Who Had Excuses

O my Lord, I am not eloquent…
I am slow of speech and slow of tongue.

EXODUS 4:10

Moses's place of significance in the Bible is evident from the more than 800 verses in Scripture that refer to him. His first 40 years of life were spent in Egypt, where he received his name—meaning "drawn out"—from Pharaoh's daughter, who had drawn him out of a basket floating on the waters of the Nile River. God sovereignly protected this son of a Hebrew slave, and Moses was given the greatest education of the ancient world—at the court of the great Pharaoh. But at age 40, his life was changed forever when he killed an Egyptian for harming an Israelite slave (Exodus 2:12). Moses then fled for his life and spent the next 40 years in the desert as a humble shepherd.

At age 80, Moses the sheepherder gave excuse after excuse to God when the Lord called him to "bring My people…out of Egypt" (Exodus 3:10). *There must be a mistake*, Moses might have thought. He wasn't the right man for this job. After all, he was just an ordinary man, a shepherd! In response, Moses gave five reasons why he was not qualified (Exodus 3:11–4:13).

Dear man of God, the Lord has a purpose and plan for your life as well. But if you, like Moses, cling to your weaknesses, doubts, and excuses, you will never know or fulfill God's will. What is God asking of you that may be out of your comfort zone? Whatever it is, know that God never asks anything of you without giving you the resources to complete the task. Cling to this powerful verse for assurance: "I can do all things through Christ who strengthens me" (Philippians 4:13). Remember this: You can't, but He can!

A Man Who Let Pride Be a Barrier

Are not...the rivers of Damascus,
better than all the waters of Israel?
Could I not wash in them and be clean?

2 KINGS 5:12

Naaman was a great military leader who had a great problem—he was "a leper" (2 Kings 5:1). Leprosy was a severe handicap and a dreaded and incurable disease. In desperation, Naaman willingly listened to the suggestion of a young Israelite slave girl who served his wife. According to this servant, Naaman should go to the prophet Elisha, who could help him. Naaman was expecting that the prophet would be impressed by the fact such a great leader had come to him. Instead, the general was told to "go and wash in the Jordan seven times, and...you shall be clean" (verse 10).

Naaman had come to Elisha to find a cure for his leprosy, but on his own terms. He was willing to go so far as to visit the prophet, but when he heard what he was to do, his pride stopped him. He reasoned, "Are not...the rivers of Damascus, better than all the waters of Israel? Could I not wash in them and be clean?" Naaman then went "away in a rage" (verse 12). The issue was not the water, but his obedience to God's instructions. Fortunately, Naaman had devoted servants who were willing to point out his pride. Only after Naaman humbled himself and washed in the Jordan was he cured. Then he said, "There is no God in all the earth, except in Israel" (verse 15).

Pride is a deceptive attitude, and it's one that we are rarely willing to recognize and confess. It is a sin of self-will—it is often the last hurdle between us and God's will. Maybe that's why God hates pride (Proverbs 6:17). It is a sin every person succumbs to, a sin we must beware of. Like Naaman, pay attention to those who encourage you and plead with you to do the right thing. Listen to wise counsel. Don't let pride stand in the way of your relationships, especially with God. Confess your pride and be washed clean of this ugly sin.

A Man Who Prayed About Everything

So it was, when I heard these words,
that I sat down and wept,
and mourned for many days;
I was fasting and praying
before the God of heaven.

NEHEMIAH 1:4

When Nehemiah heard about the condition of the broken-down wall around Jerusalem, he not only "sat down and wept, and mourned for many days," but he also fasted and prayed before God. Like other devout Jews, Nehemiah spent time each day facing toward Jerusalem while praying to God. Upon hearing the news about Jerusalem, Nehemiah repeatedly and fervently prayed about the people and the city.

Are you passionate about prayer, praying about everything? Or are your prayers a bit lopsided as you pray for things to go your way? Do you pray "I want…" and "Give me…" prayers rather than "Help me to…" prayers? There are definitely right and wrong ways to pray, and one of the wrong ways is to ask for things for the wrong reasons.

When you pray, be sure to lift your motives before the Lord and ask Him to search your heart.

The Bible urges us to pray frequently, fervently, always, constantly, without ceasing, and in and about everything. If you are new to prayer, or you want to improve your prayer life, put these biblical principles for prayer to use:

- When you pray, realize you are talking with God Himself.

- When you pray, examine your heart's condition and desires. Willingly acknowledge any sinful motives and adjust them. Do what you must to have your requests match up with what God says is pleasing to Him.

- As you pray for yourself, your loved ones, and your life's issues, be sure to pray for the concerns and needs of other people too.

Pursue prayer, and reap the blessings of seeing God's will done both in and around you.

A Man Who Answered His Own Prayer

…when I heard these words…
I sat down and wept,
and mourned for many days;
I was fasting and praying
before the God of heaven.

NEHEMIAH 1:4

Nehemiah was a trusted cupbearer to King Artaxerxes of Persia. Ninety years had passed since the first group of Jews had returned to Jerusalem from captivity. Through a messenger, Nehemiah received distressing news of the state of affairs in Jerusalem: God's people were struggling to fend off threats from hostile neighbors because the wall had not been rebuilt after its destruction.

Needless to say, Nehemiah was greatly disturbed when he heard that Jerusalem was in such a sad condition. Aware that the neglect of rebuilding the wall was a sin issue as much as a survival issue, he prayed and fasted for the next five months! And, as Nehemiah prayed, he realized that God had put him in a strategic place to take on the task of helping to rebuild the wall. As the king's trusted cupbearer, he had access to the king and to resources to help. Nehemiah's prayers helped him to expand his horizons and recognize his own usefulness. He came to understand that he could have a role in helping to answer his prayers.

God communicated a need to Nehemiah through a message, which resulted in Nehemiah's prayers and his becoming a part of the answer to those prayers. Similarly, God communicates to you as the Holy Spirit speaks to your heart when you read His Word. Then, as you pray, you can communicate to God your hopes, dreams, and burdens. What "Jerusalem" or problem is on your heart? Allow God to expand your vision as to how that burden can be lifted. You just might be part of the answer to your own prayer. Or you may learn that God is directing your resources and contributions elsewhere. Regardless, prayer is always the starting point for understanding God's will for your life.

A Man Who Had a Plan

*Then the king said to me, "What do you request?"
… "If it pleases the king…send me to Judah…
that I may rebuild it."*

NEHEMIAH 2:4-5

Nehemiah was a man of prayer. And it was as he prayed about the needs of the people in Jerusalem that he began to realize his personal responsibility. Answering the prayers was God's part, but planning was to be Nehemiah's part. When you read about Nehemiah's preparations (Nehemiah 1:1–2:10), two types of men come to mind:

Type 1 Men don't plan. They think they have plans, but in reality all they have are ideas that they're not willing to bring to fruition. They drift through life, bouncing from pillar to post. Normally those who don't plan don't prosper, whereas "the plans of the diligent lead surely to plenty" (Proverbs 21:5). And it's a long-time adage that "planning ahead will get you ahead."

If you are a Type 1 Man, now is the time to start. It's as simple as making a list of things you need to do today, tomorrow, next week, next month, and next year. If you don't plan your day, you can be sure nothing will happen.

Be the master of your day—and your life—by planning and mastering your plan for your every day.

Type 2 Men do plan. For them, planning is a lifestyle. These men have lists, schedules, and goals. And they produce results. Wherever they place their focus and attention, things get done. Progress is made.

It's good to be a Type 2 Man, but you also want to make sure your primary focus is not on the things of this world, but the things that are of eternal value—things like a closer relationship with God and family. If you are a Type 2 Man—a person who plans—evaluate your focus. Make sure that you plan time with God, time in worship, and lots of time with your family. These are the things that really matter.

A Man Who Could Motivate Others

*I told them of the hand of my God
which had been good upon me, and also of
the king's words that he had spoken to me.
So they said, "Let us rise up and build."*

NEHEMIAH 2:18

Nehemiah was a leader without followers. He had all the right credentials and the material resources, but he needed help. Rebuilding the wall around Jerusalem was a massive project that no one had been able to accomplish for 90 years. How was Nehemiah going to get the wall rebuilt at last? He would have to motivate others to help!

To his credit, Nehemiah did not dwell on the difficulties of the gargantuan project or the sacrifice that the people would face while rebuilding the wall. They had already been immobilized by hurdles for 90 years. Instead, Nehemiah directed the people's gaze to the golden opportunities of the future. He pointed to solutions, not problems. He said, "Come and let us build the wall of Jerusalem, that we may no longer be a reproach" (2:17). The people responded, "Let us rise up and build" (verse 18). They responded to the opportunity to no longer be oppressed by their hostile neighbors.

Motiving others starts in your own life. You cannot light a fire in another person's heart until a fire has been ignited in your own. To motivate people, you need to first get yourself in gear and start moving forward. If you want to instill intrinsic motivation—motivation from within—in others, you must begin by stirring your own inner desire to press forward. You must first kindle a fire in your own heart.

There is no growth in the status quo. A life of ease may sound appealing, but slowly and steadily you will lose your motivation and your muscle. Your potential will lose its momentum and diminish. To challenge and motivate others, you must first be challenged and motivated yourself. A challenge will cause you to grow. It will test your skills and transform you from today's average guy to tomorrow's leader who can motivate others to accomplish great things.

A Man Who Possessed Integrity

Remember me, my God, for good,
according to all that I have done for this people.

NEHEMIAH 5:19

The fact that Nehemiah was trusted as a king's cupbearer gives us insight into his sterling character. The greatest leader in the world at that time, King Artaxerxes of Persia, would have needed to select a man who was wise, discreet, honest, and extremely loyal to be one of his closest associates. In addition, if the king was wise, he would want this man to be intellectually capable and emotionally mature. The autobiography that bears Nehemiah's name confirms that Nehemiah was truly a man of character.

In Nehemiah chapter 5, you witness Nehemiah's personal integrity and compassion. They serve as a model of godly behavior as he confronted the nobles and rulers who were exploiting the poor people in Jerusalem. Nehemiah never demanded special privileges, and he never took money from the people. Instead, he paid for his personal expenses out of his own pocket. He looked to God as the ultimate and final judge of his integrity as he ended his story with these words: "Remember me, O my God, concerning this…" (13:14).

Nehemiah's example gives you a picture of what integrity looks like. Integrity will…

- reinforce and protect your moral convictions;
- give you a source of accountability;
- provide you with a set of standards;
- require you to make the harder and more courageous decisions; and as a bonus,
- draw those around you to a higher moral standard.

Integrity means doing the right thing even when no one is watching. That's why you must stay close to Jesus as He guides your every step. Your integrity is based on doing what is right—one decision at a time. It takes a lifetime to gain people's trust, and that can be destroyed with one mistake, one lapse in judgment, one poor decision. As you faithfully look to God through prayer and His Word, He will lead you through the decisions you need to make.

A Man Who Walked with God

Noah found grace
in the eyes of the LORD.
GENESIS 6:8

The Bible reports that nine generations after God created Adam and Eve, mankind grew so evil that God determined to destroy the human race (Genesis 6:13). But in the midst of rampant sin, violence, and corruption, one man, named Noah, stood out brilliantly as the only godly person on the face of the earth, for "Noah walked with God" (Genesis 6:9).

God graciously spared Noah and his family from His plan to flood the earth. He told Noah to build an ark for protection from the coming destruction. Noah did as God commanded, and according to the instructions, he put animals in the ark—two by two, male and female. The flood came and destroyed all living creatures on the earth. After the flood receded and the ark rested upon Mount Ararat, Noah and his family were allowed to leave the ark. God placed a rainbow in the sky as a sign of His promise to never again destroy the earth with a flood.

God had spared Noah and his family from judgment

because of Noah's godliness, demonstrating His compassion for those who are faithful to Him.

Today, God is still looking for righteous and obedient men, men with godly character. When He finds them, he uses them in powerful and extraordinary ways. Make whatever changes you must to ensure you are walking with God. To help you with your spiritual growth, read and study the list of godly character qualities found in 1 Timothy 3 and Titus 1. By faith, do whatever it takes to faithfully follow God. Noah was a light in a dark world. Follow Noah's example and serve as a light in your dark world. Be a Noah to your generation!

A Man Who Listened to the Wrong People

He rejected the advice which the elders had given him, and consulted the young men who had grown up with him.

1 KINGS 12:8

King Solomon was the wisest man on earth. The nation of Israel experienced peace and unparalleled prosperity during his lifetime and was the envy of its neighboring nations. But in order to finance this utopia, King Solomon had increased taxes to the point where most citizens were near financial ruin. By the time of his death, Solomon's extravagant lifestyle had nearly bankrupted Israel.

As was the tradition, the 12 tribes of Israel came together to anoint Solomon's successor, which was to be Rehoboam. However, what was meant to be a simple coronation became a confrontation as the northern tribes asked Rehoboam to "lighten the burdensome service"—to reduce the taxes—that his father Solomon had required. If Rehoboam would do that one thing, the northern tribes would serve him (1 Kings 12:4).

Rehoboam listened to the people, then sought the advice

of the elders who had served his father, Solomon. Their counsel was to lower the tax rate. But King Rehoboam rejected their insight and instead, took the advice of "the young men who had grown up with him." They said to increase the tax burden even more. This decision led to a divided kingdom.

Like Rehoboam, you could easily seek advice that affirms what you want to do. You can also be tempted to listen to the counsel of a loved one or a best friend who wants to help you out by supporting whatever action you desire. But first you should wait, search the Scriptures, and pray. Then you will be ready to evaluate the advice you receive with a much better frame of reference. Your decision is more likely to be one based on wisdom, not emotion. Then you can proceed because you have followed the advice of Proverbs 16:3: "Commit your works to the Lord, and your thoughts will be established."

A Man Who Lived on the Edge

O Lord GOD, remember me, I pray!
Strengthen me, I pray, just this once, O God…
JUDGES 16:28

Samson was one of the most famous judges God appointed to protect Israel from enemy nations. God promised a barren couple, Manoah and his wife, that they would have a son, and said that he was to be set apart for the Lord's use all his life. Unfortunately, as Samson grew up, he used his abilities mostly for his own selfish purposes. Yet in the end, God did use Samson to save Israel from the Philistines. Samson's final act of service was to ask God for the strength to push down the pillars of a Philistine temple. God responded, and Samson was able to push the pillars with all his might so that the entire temple came crashing down, killing him and 3,000 Philistines.

Samson served as a judge of Israel for 20 years. He was a slave to his own passions and pride. However great his gifts were, his flaws and the misuse of those gifts were greater. Samson chose to see how close he could get to the edge of obedience by forming compromising relationships and involving himself with questionable people and activities.

Though Samson was incredibly strong, he fell short of living up to his potential because of his selfish pursuits.

You too have great potential and access to remarkable spiritual power from the Lord. Choose to live up to that potential. Rather than seeing how close you can live to the edge of obedience by making questionable choices or associating with those who are likely to bring you down to their level of sinful conduct, see how close you can stay to God's standards as revealed in the Bible. Let these words from Scripture be your safeguard: "Your word I have hidden in my heart, that I might not sin against You" (Psalm 119:11). Your life has untapped potential. Let the heavenly potter fashion it for His use.

A Man Who Was Faithful

*Far be it from me
that I should sin against the LORD
in ceasing to pray for you;
but I will teach you
the good and the right way.*

1 SAMUEL 12:23

Samuel's godliness and commitment were nurtured even before his birth when his godly mother, Hannah, dedicated her yet-to-be born son to the Lord. Hannah's passion for God was passed on to Samuel during his first three to five years of childhood before he was left at the tabernacle to serve God. From his early youth, Samuel's devotion to God and his concern for the people established him as an authentic spokesman for the Lord.

Throughout his life, Samuel remained fully committed to God. He became Israel's greatest judge, and also functioned as a priest and a prophet. In all he did, Samuel showed himself to be a man who was faithful. He had a marked influence on his people as they made the transition to a new form of government. Samuel was faithful…

- to the priest, Eli, his teacher
- to God as a judge and prophet
- to the people as God's steward of the truth
- to pray for the people

Faithfulness is a lost trait for many people today. Commitments are easily broken. Responsibilities are neglected. And marriage vows have little or no meaning. But as a Christian man, faithfulness should be the center of your character. After all, one of the fruit of the Spirit is "faithfulness," which marks God's presence in your life (Galatians 5:22). Jesus showed the seriousness of being faithful in His parable of the talents. There He spoke the ultimate statement of praise: "Well done, good and faithful servant; you have been faithful over a few things, I will make you ruler over many things. Enter into the joy of your lord" (Matthew 25:23).

Pray to follow in the footsteps of Samuel and be counted as one who is "found faithful" (1 Corinthians 4:1-2).

A Man Who Did Things His Way

To obey is better than sacrifice…

1 SAMUEL 15:22

God used prophets to speak to the people of Israel for Him, and to lead them. But in time, the people wanted a human king so they could be more like the surrounding nations. This did not please the prophet Samuel, for their request for a human king meant they were rejecting God, their divine King.

The man God chose to be the first king over His people was Saul, the son of Kish, of the tribe of Benjamin. Saul was exactly what the people wanted—a physically imposing man who stood head and shoulders above all the others. After his coronation, Saul achieved early military victories that helped solidify his support among the people. But all too soon, Saul began to collapse under the pressure of leadership. This breakdown resulted from his inability to trust God and an unwillingness to obey God. Ultimately, Saul simply wouldn't do what God had commanded. God thus rejected Saul as king, but Saul continued to rule, and did so for a total of 40 years.

Saul serves as a sad and frightening illustration of the

consequences of unrepentant sin and a failure to live by God's standards. He was unwilling to do things God's way. He always had "a better idea," and when confronted, he always had excuses for his wrong actions.

God does not want us to come up with our own innovative ways of obeying Him. And He doesn't want excuses, rationalizations, or superficial shows of repentance. As Samuel told Saul, "Behold, to obey is better than sacrifice, and to heed than the fat of rams. For rebellion is as the sin of witchcraft, and stubbornness is as iniquity and idolatry" (1 Samuel 15:22-23). Are there any areas of your life in which you are failing to submit to God's rule? God wants your *complete* obedience—without excuses.

A Man Who Became a Fool

King Solomon loved many foreign women…
of whom the LORD had said to the
children of Israel, "…they will turn away
your hearts after their gods."

1 KINGS 11:1-2

Solomon was born with incredible privilege: His father was the king, and he was the heir to the throne. In addition, he was granted several encounters with God through dreams. Solomon made a good decision early in his reign and asked God for wisdom to rule rather wealth and a long life. God was pleased with Solomon's request and gave him both wisdom and wealth!

But unlike his father David, Solomon did not remain committed to the Lord throughout his life. Solomon's foreign wives did as the Bible warned: They turned his heart toward other gods. Even though Solomon was wise, he became a fool through these forbidden relationships and marriages. After his death, Solomon's kingdom was split into two nations—the northern and southern kingdoms. Solomon's life began with great promise, but ended with tragic consequences.

Solomon may have been exceedingly wise, but that didn't insulate him from making foolish choices that led to unfaithfulness to God. It might have been politically correct for him to forge alliances with the surrounding pagan nations through marriages, but it was spiritual suicide. Ultimately, Solomon's choice to have foreign wives turned him away from God. The Bible states, "The fear of the LORD is the beginning of knowledge, but fools despise wisdom and instruction" (Proverbs 1:7). With each wife, Solomon strayed farther and farther from God, despising the very wisdom that God had given him.

Choosing the right friends and relationships is extremely important for growth and maturity in the Christian life. The Bible is right on when it says associations with evil people corrupt good morals (1 Corinthians 15:33 NASB). Don't do as Solomon did and cultivate relationships based on expediency or passion. Choose friends who challenge you to greater spiritual growth, who pull you up and encourage you in your Christian life. Ask God to guide you to those people who will help you stay close to Him.

A Man Who Was Honorable

*…the servants of my lord
are encamped in the open fields.
Shall I then go to my house
to eat and drink…?
I will not do this thing.*

2 SAMUEL 11:11

U riah was a soldier in the Israelite army. In fact, he was listed in 2 Samuel 23:8 as "one of the mighty men whom David had"—one of 37 of the bravest and most outstanding warriors in David's army. Uriah would be the equivalent of an Army Ranger, a Force Recon Marine, or a Navy SEAL in our modern-day fighting forces. He was among the best of the best, and he knew where he was supposed to be—fighting for King David on the front line against the Ammonites.

As the king, David should have been on that same battlefield, but he had chosen to stay in Jerusalem. One day while out walking, he saw Uriah's wife bathing on a roof below his palace. He asked who she was and learned that she was married to Uriah, one of his most trusted men. Yet in his lust, David slept with Bathsheba, and she became pregnant.

David thought he could cover up his indiscretion with Bathsheba by having Uriah recalled from the battle so he would spend time at home with his wife. But Uriah did not believe it was right for him to be with Bathsheba while his men were fighting the enemy. Because of Uriah's integrity, David decided to have him killed. He had Uriah put out in front of the battle, and then had the army withdraw, leaving Uriah to die at the hands of the enemy. Uriah's honor cost him his life, but it also enshrined him in God's record book as a man who would not compromise his commitments.

Stand for something, or you will fall for anything. Honor, integrity, and commitment should be at the very core of your being. Open your heart to God and let Him shape you and fill you with His Word and His principles. Ask God to guard and guide your every thought and decision, to make you a man who upholds His standards—a man after God's own heart.

A Man Whose Life Ended Badly

When [Uzziah] was strong
his heart was lifted up, to his destruction,
for he transgressed
against the LORD his God.

2 CHRONICLES 26:16

U zziah was 16 years old when he became king of Judah, and he reigned 52 years. He was described as a king who "did what was right in the sight of the LORD." Early in his reign, Uzziah sought the Lord and was successful in his military campaigns. He was also known for the development of weaponry and his supervision over many building projects. During the years that he sought the Lord, he and the nation of Judah prospered.

Toward the end of his life, Uzziah became proud of all that he had accomplished. Forgetting that God was the source of all his success, Uzziah decided he no longer needed an intermediary between himself and God, and he brashly entered the temple and attempted to burn incense before the Lord. For this act of disobedience, God struck him with leprosy.

Another king, Nebuchadnezzar of Babylon, succumbed

to pride as well and boasted, "Is not this great Babylon, that I have built for a royal dwelling by my mighty power and for the honor of my majesty?" (Daniel 4:30). Like Uzziah, Nebuchadnezzar was judged for his pride and arrogant spirit.

Uzziah's arrogance should be a reminder to all people of the danger of becoming prideful. His example also points out the fact that a lifetime of wise living can be marred by a single moment of unwise behavior. The Christian life is not a sprint; it's a marathon. Ask God for the grace and wisdom to finish the race with humility and obedience. Imprint this verse on your heart and mind to help you finish the Christian race victoriously: "Be careful how you live. Don't live like fools, but like those who are wise. Make the most of every opportunity in these evil days. Don't act thoughtlessly, but understand what the Lord wants you to do" (Ephesians 5:15-17 NLT).

NEW TESTAMENT MEN

A Man Who Brought Others to Jesus

He [Andrew] first found his own brother Simon, and said to him, "We have found the Messiah."

JOHN 1:41

As a disciple of John the Baptist, Andrew was directed by John to Jesus as the "the Lamb of God" (John 1:36). Andrew then brought his brother, Simon, to Jesus, telling Simon, "We have found the Messiah" (verse 41). Andrew and his brother Simon returned to their fishing business until John the Baptist was imprisoned. After that, the two brothers went on to become part of the 12 disciples.

During one of Jesus's preaching tours, a multitude made up of 5,000-plus men needed food (John 6:10). Andrew brought a boy to Jesus, saying, "There is a lad here who has five barley loaves and two fish…but what are these for so many people?" (verse 9). Jesus then miraculously multiplied the loaves and fishes and fed all the people—and still had several baskets of food left over.

Andrew was diligent about introducing people to Jesus. In John 12:22, we read about a group of Greeks he brought to Jesus. After Jesus ascended into heaven, Andrew was among those who continued teaching in Jerusalem. According to tradition, Andrew continued bringing people to Jesus all throughout Asia Minor and Greece, until he was martyred.

For most men, sharing the gospel is a frightening thing. They are unsure of how to talk about Jesus and Christianity, so they don't say anything. Andrew is a good role model for us. More specifically, Andrew simply brought people to Jesus, and He let Jesus do the rest.

As a believer, follow Andrew's example and introduce people to Jesus. The men you associate with on a daily basis have needs that only Jesus can satisfy. Share how Jesus has changed your life. Let your spiritually hungry friends know about Jesus, who is "the bread of life" (John 6:35).

A Man Who Was Willing to Learn

Now a certain Jew named Apollos…
[was] an eloquent man and mighty in the
Scriptures.

ACTS 18:24

The apostle Paul was a Jew who traveled throughout the Roman world sharing the good news of Jesus Christ. Each town he visited, he would speak to fellow Jews at their synagogue. When his message was rejected, Paul would then preach to the Gentiles in the area. There were also Gentile ministers in the Roman world who preached in established churches made up of both Jews and Gentiles. Apollos was one of these Gentiles, "an eloquent man and mighty in the Scriptures."

Apollos was knowledgeable about the Old Testament and a gifted speaker. As a result, he was able to refute the Jews in their synagogues. The only problem with Apollos's message was that it was incomplete: He "knew only of the baptism of John" (Acts 18:25). He knew of Jesus as the Messiah, but did not understand the significance of Christ's atoning death and resurrection or the ministry of the Holy Spirit.

Today, many men are content with their present level of knowledge. They are satisfied with the status quo and believe they don't need any more information. Unlike these men, Apollos was not content. When Aquila and Priscilla, tentmakers and companions of the apostle Paul, heard Apollos speak and noticed his incomplete knowledge, they took him aside and "explained to him the way of God more accurately" (verse 26). Amazingly, the brilliant Apollos listened and learned from these simple tentmakers.

Apollos was willing to learn. How about you? Do you have a learner's spirit? Are you a man who continues to learn and grow, whether it is for your job or your spiritual growth and maturity? One of the best ways to continue learning is to be a reader, starting with your Bible. You will also want to read Christian books that will help you with your personal life and your role as a husband, father, leader, and witness for Christ to the world. God is able to use a man who is a learner.

A Man Who Was a Team Player

Greet Priscilla and Aquila, my fellow workers in Christ Jesus, who risked their own necks for my life, to whom not only I give thanks, but also all the churches of the Gentiles.

ROMANS 16:3

Marriage is often described as a team sport because it takes two people to make it happen. One of the premiere examples of this is Aquila and his wife Priscilla. In the pages of the New Testament, their names are always mentioned together, and they were a force to be reckoned with in terms of ministry.

Aquila was originally from Pontus, an area by the Black Sea. Eventually he and Priscilla ended up meeting each other in the Greek city of Corinth. While there, they began to work with the apostle Paul. What can we learn from Aquila?

- Aquila had a trade. As a Jew, Aquila had been taught to be a tentmaker. He worked hard and provided for his wife.

- Aquila was hospitable. After Paul met Aquila and Priscilla, Aquila invited Paul to live with him and his wife. This hospitality lasted for more than a year while they were still in Corinth.

- Aquila was teachable. From the moment he met Paul, he became an avid student of God's Word. As Aquila grew in knowledge, he became more useful in ministry, to the point of giving further instruction to the evangelist Apollos (Acts 18:26).

- Aquila was available. When Paul decided to go to Ephesus (verse 18), Aquila and Priscilla packed up and went with Paul. Later, when needed, Aquila and his wife moved to Rome, where they started a church.

- Aquila was a team player. He worked well with Paul in ministry, and he was not threatened by the gifts and abilities of his wife, Priscilla. He saw her as his complement, and together they had an incredible team ministry.

To follow Aquila's example,

be diligent in your work,

be available to help in ministry,

be teachable,

be a team player in ministry—especially with your wife, and

be an encourager to your wife, unthreatened by her gifts for ministry.

A Man Who Encouraged Others

*And Joses, who was also named Barnabas
by the apostles (which is translated Son of
Encouragement)…brought the money and laid it
at the apostles' feet.*

ACTS 4:36-37

Did you have a nickname as a child? Or do you have one now as an adult? Either way, your nickname is probably related to some characteristic about you, right? Well, Joses must have had a significant ministry to the members of the early church because the apostles observed his actions and gave him the name *Barnabas*, meaning "Son of Encouragement."

We first meet Barnabas as he encouraged the members of the Jerusalem church by selling his land and giving the money for the needs of the members. Next we see him interceding on Saul's behalf after Saul declared himself to be a Christian (Acts 9:26-27). After that, Barnabas traveled to a newly planted church in Antioch and "encouraged them all that with purpose of heart they should continue with the Lord" (11:23). And still later, Barnabas sought a more gifted teacher to help mature the Antioch church by traveling to Tarsus to find Paul and bring him back (11:25-26).

It has been said, "Any fool can tell you ten things you are doing wrong." In Barnabas, however, we meet a rare person who looked for ways to build up and strengthen others. According to Proverbs 25:11, "A word fitly spoken is like apples of gold in settings of silver."

In daily life, our tendency is to focus on ourselves. But when we look around, we will quickly discover there are many people who could use encouragement. Decide to be supportive and constructive with your words and actions, starting in your own home. Your family needs your "fitly spoken" words. Then move outward and bless others. Encouragement offered at the right moment can mean the difference between someone finishing well or collapsing along the way. Like Barnabas, you will be a blessing to those you encourage.

A Man Who Was Different

There was a certain man...called Cornelius,
a centurion...a devout man and one who
feared God.

ACTS 10:1-2

Today we have the joy and privilege of meeting a military man who was a devout follower of God. He must have stood out as a godly man because the book of Acts mentions him as a positive example for all men. Meet Cornelius!

Cornelius was not just any soldier; he was one of 60 officers in a legion of 6,000 men. He was a leader who commanded 100 men. Cornelius was different because he had abandoned the pagan religion of his nation and worshipped the true God of the Jews. He "feared God" and led his whole family to do the same—to fear and revere the God of Israel. But the extent of Cornelius's religious zeal had yet to be realized. When the apostle Peter arrived at his house and presented the gospel message of Jesus Christ, God opened the officer's heart to respond, and Cornelius and all those in his household were converted to Christianity.

In Cornelius's high-ranking position in Roman circles, there's no doubt he faced enormous pressures to engage in the activities of pagan culture. We live in a similar world today—a world that is constantly trying to conform us into its image. Secular society does not want you to be different. How can you keep from caving in to the world's pressure? The Bible gives this solution: "Do not be conformed to this world, but be transformed by the renewing of your mind" (Romans 12:2). To be different, you must consistently seek the strength God's Word can give you to stand firm each day. With the Spirit's help, you will not be conformed to the world's thinking, but your heart and mind will be transformed so that you are like Cornelius: "a devout man and one who feared God," a man who is different!

A Man Who Was Self-Important

I wrote to the church, but Diotrephes,
who loves to have the preeminence among them,
does not receive us.

3 JOHN 9

Fifty years after the resurrection and ascension of Jesus, all of the apostles were dead except John. Even at his advanced age, John was actively involved in overseeing the churches of Asia Minor. At that time, church leaders traveled from town to town to help establish new churches and strengthen the existing ones. In a letter John wrote to one church, he commended two men and condemned the self-serving ministry of a third man, Diotrephes.

Diotrephes was guilty of unjustly accusing the apostle John of false and evil statements. In his pride, Diotrephes turned away traveling church leaders, and those who tried to welcome and accept these leaders were removed from the church by Diotrephes (3 John 10).

Pride, jealousy, slander, and ambition are common qualities in the secular world, where a lot of people will do whatever is necessary to get even or get ahead. But humility, not pride, should be the prevailing attitude of those who are in the church.

Self-importance, which is actually pride, can easily creep into your heart and mind if you are not careful. Pride can blind you to your own faults and magnify the faults of others. Because it is so devious, pride is usually one of the last sins we confess. To defend yourself against pride, follow Jesus's example: He "humbled Himself by becoming obedient to the point of death" (Philippians 2:8). Pray the prayer found in Luke 18:13: "God, be merciful to me, a sinner!" Ask God to help you search for pride within your heart so you will not do as Diotrephes did and desire and love preeminence among other people.

A Man Who Was Honored

Receive him therefore in the Lord with all gladness, and hold such men in esteem.

PHILIPPIANS 2:29

E paphroditus was a Gentile who grew up in a pagan home, where he received a name that meant "belonging to Aphrodite" or "Venus." When the apostle Paul arrived in Philippi and discovered there was no Jewish synagogue, he went to the place where "God-fearers" prayed. There, he found a group of women who were willing to hear the message of Jesus and became believers. This was the beginning of the church in Philippi.

About ten years later, when the Philippian church heard about Paul's imprisonment in Rome, they sent Epaphroditus with gifts to help Paul. After arriving in Rome, Epaphroditus became sick and almost died. Word got back to Philippi of Epaphroditus's illness, and Epaphroditus was distressed because he thought he had failed in his mission. Paul then wrote a letter to the church in Philippi, assuring the people that Epaphroditus's mission had not failed. Rather, the opposite had occurred. A healthy Epaphroditus then returned home, carrying with him the epistle to the

Philippians. Within the letter, Epaphroditus received high praise from Paul as "a brother, fellow worker, and fellow soldier" (Philippians 2:25).

How would you evaluate your motivation at work or at church? Do you seek the praise, affirmation, and honor of others? As Christ's man, your efforts should have the highest of motivations: "Therefore, whether you eat or drink, or whatever you do, do all to the glory of God" (1 Corinthians 10:31). Your mission is to humbly serve and please God, not to seek the honor of men.

Like Epaphroditus, serve others faithfully to the glory of God. And when your time on earth is done, you will be able to stand before your Lord and receive the greatest honor of all, which is to hear Him say, "Well done, good and faithful servant; you were faithful over a few things... Enter into the joy of your lord" (Matthew 25:21).

A Man Who Had Faith

My daughter has just died,
but come and lay Your hand on her
and she will live.

MATTHEW 9:18

Jairus must have loved his daughter very much to show such great humility and bow down before Jesus. He was an official, which meant he had social standing in the community. Because he was a leader in the local synagogue, he was used to people bowing before him. But out of love for his daughter, he gladly fell at the feet of Jesus, believing that the Lord could raise up his dead daughter.

When Jairus and Jesus arrived at the house, there were many people there who were mourning. Jesus said, "Go away. The girl is not dead but asleep" (verse 24). The Lord laid His hand on her, and she came back to life!

"Do not be afraid; only believe" (Mark 5:36). That's what Jesus told this desperate father. The different accounts of this miracle have the daughter either dead or dying when Jairus fell at Jesus's feet. But what really matters here was the faith exhibited by Jairus. His was a faith that overcame the pride of his social position and sought help for his little girl. His faith gave him the unashamed freedom to fall before Jesus with complete assurance that Jesus could help his daughter. Read how the Bible describes faith: "Without faith it is impossible to please Him, for he who comes to God must believe that He is, and that He is a rewarder of those who diligently seek Him" (Hebrews 11:6). That is saving faith—a faith that is able to accept humiliation, ridicule, and rejection and stand strong.

Ask God to give you the kind of faith Jairus showed—a faith that believes that Jesus is the answer to your every need. Jesus is asking the same thing of you that He asked of Jairus: "Do not be afraid; only believe."

A Man Who Would Be Great

Whoever desires to become great among you,
let him be your servant.

MATTHEW 20:26

James and his brother John were recruited by Jesus to follow Him. These brothers and their mother, along with the other ten disciples, followed the Lord on his way to His death in Jerusalem. Being ambitious for her sons, the mother asked Jesus, "Grant that these two sons of mine may sit, one on Your right hand and the other on the left, in Your kingdom" (Matthew 20:21). Then the sons chimed in and said, "Grant us that we may sit, one on Your right hand and the other on Your left, in Your glory" (Mark 10:37).

These requests reveal how little Jesus's message of humility had penetrated the hearts and minds of James and John and their mother. They had completely ignored Jesus's repeated message that He was going to Jerusalem to die. James and John were still thinking that Christ would set up an earthly kingdom, and they were busily maneuvering for places of prominence.

Do you view greatness the same way as James and John?

Today, as in Bible times, leadership is often seen as the exertion of force and dominance. But Jesus taught just the opposite. You are to lead as a servant—whether in your family, or at church, or in the business world. Jesus used Himself as an example of servant leadership when He said, "The Son of Man did not come to be served, but to serve" (Matthew 20:28).

For a better understanding of what biblical leadership looks like, read 1 Timothy 3:1-13 and Titus 1:5-9. As you read these about the characteristics of biblical leadership, notice that nothing is ever said about being great. These scriptures describe a man's inner life and his character, not how he leads. A godly man will be a godly leader.

A Man Who Needed Proof

Even His brothers did not believe in Him.
JOHN 7:5

James was the son of Mary and Joseph and the half-brother of Jesus Christ. According to Matthew 13:55, James was the eldest after Jesus, and there were three other brothers and at least two sisters in the family. The book of John makes it clear that throughout Jesus's life and ministry, James was an unbelieving skeptic. It wasn't until after the resurrection that Jesus singled out James and James became a believer (1 Corinthians 15:7). Once James's doubts were settled, his commitment was unmatched, and he quickly emerged as a respected church leader in Jerusalem along with the apostles.

James was a man of wisdom and gave good counsel about how Gentiles should be treated in the church (Acts 15). Later, James again demonstrated his wisdom when he wrote about the practical nature of faith by writing the short New Testament letter that bears his name. It was James who said, "Show me your faith without your works, and I will show you my faith by my works…faith without works is dead" (James 2:18-20). For James, faith was action. And who better to write about faith in action than James, who spent his life watching the daily life of his half-brother, Jesus, God in human flesh!

How many skeptics like James do you have in your life—in your family, at work, or in your circle of friends and your neighborhood? Unlike James, these people will not be visited by the resurrected Lord Jesus Christ. Instead, they will be exposed to *you*, one of Jesus's disciples! Has your life been transformed by Jesus? If so, follow James's advice and demonstrate by your good works that your faith is real. Then pray that the Spirit of Christ will convict your unbelieving family, friends, and workmates that Jesus has truly risen from the dead and offers salvation to the lost.

A Man Whose Life Was a Work in Progress

*Lord, do you want us to command fire
to come down from heaven and consume them,
just as Elijah did?*

LUKE 9:54

John was probably the youngest of the disciples—and the most brash in his earlier years. We see confirmation of this from three incidents recorded in the Gospels, all of which illustrated his need for Jesus's transforming work in his life.

- John was selfish. John thought he and the other disciples were part of an exclusive group. When an "outsider" was successful at casting out demons in Jesus's name, John complained that he "does not follow with us." Jesus rebuked John for his bias (Luke 9:49-50).

- John was vengeful. Both John and his brother, James, were angry when a village in Samaria refused to welcome them. When they asked Jesus if they could call down fire from heaven and destroy the village, Jesus rebuked them (Luke 9:51-56).

- John was ambitious. The two brothers, John and James, teamed up with their mother to ask Jesus for positions of power in His coming kingdom. Jesus once again rebuked them and used their request as an opportunity to teach on servant leadership (Matthew 20:20-28).

But Jesus's death and resurrection changed John's life. The book of Acts and John's own writings reveal that he became a loving and patient servant of his Lord. John lived to the age of nearly 100, and his final words were his life's message: "Beloved, let us love one another" (1 John 4:7).

Your Christian life is also a work in progress. Where are you on Jesus's transformation scale? Paul described the process of spiritual growth with these words: "Do not be conformed to this world, but be transformed by the renewing of your mind" (Romans 12:2). Jesus wants to conform you into His image. It's not what or where you are today that is important, but rather what—and who— you can be when you give your life fully to Jesus. God is not finished with you yet!

A Man Who Had a Mission

Prepare the way of the LORD;
make His paths straight.

MATTHEW 3:3

John the Baptist's life story is told in all four Gospels and predicted by two Old Testament prophets. John was the son of a priest named Zacharias, and his wife, Elizabeth, who was related to Mary, the mother of Jesus. John was a fiery, passionate preacher who roamed the wilderness wearing a garment of camel's hair and eating locusts and wild honey. His mission was to prepare the way for the Messiah, Jesus. He called people to repentance, and when they responded, John baptized them in the waters of the Jordan River. He even baptized Jesus, which at first, in humility, John was reluctant to do. Jesus called John the last and the greatest of the prophets. Ultimately John was beheaded at the age of 30 by King Herod; his ministry lasted only about one year.

How important is one year of your life? Have you ever thought, *I have lots of time for* _____ ? What might have happened had John the Baptist nurtured this kind of blasé mentality about his time and days? John probably didn't know that his mission would last only one brief year, but he made sure his time counted for God.

What if you were told you had only one year to live? How would you choose to spend that priceless time? You would most likely make a few changes in your life, right? Why not set a one-year goal today? As you plan, be sure to include God. Then break down that goal to what you must do month by month, and finally to what you must do today to make your time count toward God's mission for your life. Remember, the impact of your mission is not measured in length of years, but in length of obedience.

A Man Who Knew About Jesus

And supper being ended, the devil having already put it into the heart of Judas Iscariot, Simon's son, to betray Him...

JOHN 13:2

When was the last time you met a man named Judas? Probably never, because Judas is a name that speaks of the greatest betrayal of all time. Judas was one of the 12 disciples. He lived and traveled with Jesus for three years, and heard every word Jesus spoke. He was the trusted treasurer of the group. He witnessed Jesus's miracles and literally rubbed shoulders with God. And yet after all that privileged exposure to God-in-the-flesh, he betrayed Jesus!

We cannot understand why Jesus, the omniscient God of the universe, chose Judas in the first place. But it is evident from Scripture that Jesus knew what was in Judas's heart from the beginning. Jesus warned that one of his disciples was "a devil" (John 6:70). He also mentioned at the last supper that one of the disciples would betray Him (Luke 22:21). And later in His prayer to the Father, He called Judas "the son of perdition" and described him as being "lost" (John 17:12).

The shocking story of Judas is a warning and a sobering reminder of this truth: It is possible to be involved in Christian activities and to look and act like a follower of Christ, and still be lost in your sins. Search your heart to see whether you are a for-real believer or are merely going through the motions. The Bible says, "Examine yourselves as to whether you are in the faith. Test yourselves. Do you not know yourselves, that Jesus Christ is in you?—unless indeed you are disqualified" (2 Corinthians 13:5).

What's in your heart? If you are unsure whether Jesus is your Lord, bow before Him now. Embrace Him as your Savior and Lord. Judas did not make this decision, but you can. It is this decision that will take you from merely knowing *about* Jesus and becoming one who truly *knows* Jesus.

A Man Who Contended for the Faith

I found it necessary to write to you exhorting you to contend earnestly for the faith...

JUDE 3

Jude was the youngest son of Joseph and Mary and the brother of James and the half-brother of Jesus (Matthew 13:55). Neither Jude nor his older brothers believed that Jesus was the Messiah until after His resurrection. Jude was part of the meeting of Jesus's 120 followers held in the upper room after Jesus's ascension into heaven. Jude went on to become a fervent spokesman, proclaiming Christ as God.

By the time Jude wrote the letter that bears his name, all the apostles except John had been martyred. Even though Christianity had spread throughout the Roman empire, its spiritual purity was in great jeopardy. The church was under political and spiritual attack, and Jude called for the church to fight for the truth in the midst of this great spiritual battle.

Jude was concerned about false teachers who had crept

into the churches unnoticed. Or, if these teachers had been noticed, Christians had not bothered to confront their errors. The same problem is happening in today's church. Satan does everything he can to spread false teachings. God, through Jude, is asking you "to contend earnestly for the faith." You cannot afford to stand on the sidelines while others teach falsehood and slander your Lord and His people. Defending your faith is not optional—it's a must.

The weapon you are to use to contend for the faith is the Bible. The wisdom found in it is to be desired more than gold (Proverbs 16:16). And the "word of God is living and powerful, and sharper than any two-edged sword, piercing even to the division of soul and spirit, and of joints and marrow, and is a discerner of the thoughts and intents of the heart" (Hebrews 4:12).

Determine to know the value of God's Word. Gain a better understanding of the Bible so you won't be susceptible to false teaching. With a knowledge of Scripture, you can stand strong in the defense of God's truth.

A Man Who Served Sacrificially

*Luke the beloved physician
and Demas greet you.*

COLOSSIANS 4:14

Luke was a physician by training and the only Gentile author of the books of the New Testament. Because of his education, he served as an excellent historian of the events of Jesus's life and the expansion of the church. Luke was not a distant observer, but an active participant in the rigorous and dangerous missionary journeys of Paul. He may very well have been the first medical missionary.

Luke is mentioned by name only three times in the New Testament—all three times, Paul was the writer. Paul's use of the word "beloved" in Colossians 4:14 to describe Luke tells us much about Luke's character. As a physician, Luke was trained to care for the physical needs of people. In his account of the life of Jesus in the book of Luke, we see his compassion, especially for the poor, for women, and for the despised of Jewish society. We also see Luke's concern for the apostle Paul. In spite of the many dangers and hardships faced during Paul's missionary journeys, Luke remained close to Paul to the very end of the apostle's life.

In his Gospel, Luke recorded Jesus's words that anyone who follows Him must count the cost and "deny himself, and take up his cross daily" (Luke 9:23). Luke counted the cost and chose to:

- give up his respectable profession
- suffer hardships to serve God
- spend years to compile the material for his account of Jesus's life
- minister to the apostle Paul
- write the book of Acts

Discipleship is costly. It calls for us to stop dabbling and be 100 percent committed to Jesus. Take time to pray and count the cost, and decide along with Luke that the cost is well worth any and every sacrifice. On the other side of your decision, you will find an incredible usefulness awaiting you for the cause of Christ!

A Man Who Was Given a Second Chance

*Get Mark…for he is useful
to me for ministry.*

2 TIMOTHY 4:11

Mark was the cousin of Barnabas, a leader in the early church who became an associate of the apostle Paul. Mark was asked to join Barnabas and Paul as their assistant on their first missionary journey. For some unknown reason, Mark later deserted the team and returned to Jerusalem (Acts 13:13).

Several years later, Barnabas wanted to take Mark on another missionary trip, but Paul said no (Acts 15:39). So Barnabas and Mark went to Cyprus. Years later, after Barnabas gave Mark a second chance, Mark became a useful servant to Paul. Paul wrote in his last epistle, "Get Mark and bring him with you, for he is useful to me for ministry" (2 Timothy 4:11). Not only was Mark a help to Paul, but he assisted Peter as well, who referred to Mark as "my son" while they ministered together in Rome (1 Peter 5:13). Mark recorded Peter's account of the life of Jesus in the Gospel that bears his name—the Gospel of Mark.

Failure is not the end; it is the opportunity for a new beginning. Many who have had a "Mark-like" experience in their Christian life have gone on to make significant contributions to the cause of Christ. Have you experienced a failure in your life? Most likely you have. And yet your life isn't over! Mark is a vivid example of what can happen when given a second chance, an opportunity to learn from your mistakes. When you fail, ask God to give you the courage to get up and keep going—to go another round.

Do you have a mentor who can help you? If not, ask God to bring a Barnabas-like person into your life who will believe in you and make a spiritual investment in you. God is in the business of giving second chances. Are you ready and willing to accept His offer? As happened with Mark, it's not how well you begin that's most important, but how well you finish.

A Man Who Left Everything

[Jesus] saw a man named Matthew
sitting at the tax office.
And He said to him, "Follow Me."
So he arose and followed Him.

MATTHEW 9:9

Matthew lived in Israel and was a tax collector for the Roman government. Like most of his fellow tax collectors, Matthew was a rich man, as evidenced by his first recorded act as a follower of Jesus—Matthew gave a great banquet to introduce his friends to Jesus. Matthew then became one of Jesus's 12 disciples. As an eyewitness of Jesus's life, Matthew went on to write an account of Jesus's ministry. The Gospel of Matthew became an early evangelistic tool for sharing the gospel with the Jewish communities scattered across the Roman Empire. Tradition says Matthew was burned at the stake, having given his all to follow Christ.

Of all Jesus's followers, Matthew had the most to lose. Tax collecting was a lucrative profession. Once Matthew left his job, his financial situation was drastically altered forever. There could be no turning back. Yet Matthew did not hesitate for a moment when Jesus said, "Follow Me."

Matthew counted the cost and left his secular profession. All he had was his pen, his record-keeping skills, and his friends in the secular world, whom He immediately introduced to Jesus. From that point on, Jesus gave Matthew a new use for his skills—that of keeping a record of what he observed as he followed Jesus. The Gospel that bears Matthew's name is the fruit of his ministry, and of his love for his Savior.

After you come to Christ, you too have friends who need to be introduced to Jesus. Let them see Jesus through your transformed life. And then, like Matthew, Jesus wants you to use your unique set of talents, skills, and experiences to honor Him and bless others. Like Matthew, freely give yourself to Jesus to be used however He desires.

A Man Who Was Honest

*Behold, an Israelite indeed,
in whom is no deceit!*

JOHN 1:47

Nathanael was one of Jesus's first disciples, having been brought to Jesus by Philip (John 1:43-46). As Philip and Nathanael approached Jesus, the Savior described Nathanael as a man who knew no guile or deception, a man with an honest heart. These words from the psalmist could have been used to describe Nathanael: "Blessed is the man to whom the LORD does not impute iniquity, and in whose spirit there is no deceit" (Psalm 32:2).

Nathanael acted from a pure heart, but he was not gullible. When Philip, a friend, told Nathanael that he had found the Messiah, who was from Nazareth, Nathanael reasoned, "Why would the anticipated Messiah come from a place in the middle of nowhere like Nazareth? Why not Jerusalem, the center of all religious and political activity?" (see Luke 1:46). Unconvinced but wanting to know the truth about this "Jesus," Nathanael went to see for himself.

Unfortunately, honest men are hard to find today. They have become the exception rather than the rule. Rather than follow Nathanael's example, many men follow Jacob's lifestyle of trickery and deceit (Genesis 27). It's easy to justify and excuse a less-than-honest lifestyle. After all, "everyone" does that. But the standard we should follow comes from God, not the world.

As God's man, you are called to live by the highest of standards and always be honest. You are to conscientiously avoid lies, half-truths, and omissions of the truth. Strive to be straightforward in your words and actions. And don't fall into the trap of telling people what they want to hear so you can get what you want or to get ahead. God wants you to be a trustworthy person at all times, and for others to be able to say of you what Jesus said of Nathanael: "Here is…a man of complete integrity" (NLT).

A Man Who Grew in Boldness

Nicodemus, who at first came to Jesus by night,
also came, bringing a mixture of myrrh and aloes…
JOHN 19:39

We don't know exactly when Nicodemus became a follower of Jesus, but by the time of Jesus's death, Nicodemus was fully committed to Christ. His story begins with his encounter with Jesus under the cover of darkness very early in Jesus's ministry (John 3:2). Nicodemus was a Pharisee, one of Israel's prominent religious leaders, and a member of the religious counsel known as the Sanhedrin. It would not go well for his reputation if he was seen talking to Jesus, a controversial teacher. But Nicodemus was curious about Jesus's teachings and wanting to know more.

After this less-than-bold move on Nicodemus's part, we can see definite signs of spiritual growth. In John 7, Nicodemus was criticized for attempting to defend Jesus's actions and teachings. He said, "Does our law judge a man before it hears him and knows what he is doing?" (verses 50-52). Finally, in full view of all of Jerusalem, Nicodemus and Joseph of Arimathea took a risky step and asked for Jesus's body so they could give Him a proper burial (John

19:38-40). We have no further record of Nicodemus, but most likely he was scorned, shunned, and removed from the Sanhedrin.

Being born again spiritually is instantaneous, but spiritual growth is not. The seeds of growth were deposited when the Holy Spirit took up residence in you. From that point on, you must do your part and "grow in the grace and knowledge of our Lord and Savior Jesus Christ" (2 Peter 3:18). How is this growth to proceed? Start by feasting on God's Word. Pray to be more like Jesus. And walk in obedience. You may be like Nicodemus, who was timid at first, but as you gradually become more confident and knowledgeable, you too can boldly be identified with Christ. A sure sign of how your growth is progressing will be your increasing boldness.

A Man Who Did the Right Thing

I am sending [Onesimus] back.
You therefore receive him...

PHILEMON 12

Slavery was widespread in the Roman Empire. It's been estimated that slaves constituted at least one-third of the empire's population. In Paul's day, slaves could be doctors, musicians, teachers, artists, or work in many other vocations. Some slaves enjoyed favorable situations, but there were many who were treated cruelly.

Onesimus was a slave who had robbed his master, Philemon, and then run away, hoping to lose himself in the large slave population of Rome. By God's providence, Onesimus met Paul in Rome and became a Christian. Paul quickly grew fond of Onesimus (Philemon 12,16) and wanted to keep him in Rome because of the help he provided while Paul was in prison (verse 11).

Paul urged that Onesimus return to his master, and of course Onesimus could have fled to another part of the empire. Instead, he returned to Philemon with a letter from Paul. Onesimus had broken Roman law by stealing from his master and fleeing, and now that he was a believer, he wanted to do the right thing and face the consequences of his actions.

Though Onesimus was now a believer and his past sins were forgiven, he was still obligated to answer for his actions. Onesimus showed his transformed life by willingly returning and submitting himself to his master's judgment. He understood the reality that he was free from his sins but not the consequences of them.

If you are a Christian, you have been set free from the sins of your past through the shed blood of Christ. Thank God for that freedom! Forgiveness in Christ now gives you the responsibility and freedom to do what is right. Is there something from your past that you need to make right? If so, ask God to give you the courage and strength to do whatever is necessary to repair a broken relationship or right a wrong that you committed.

A Man Who Was Unique

Paul, an apostle of Jesus Christ
by the will of God…
EPHESIANS 1:1

Paul was born in Tarsus in Asia Minor, about the same time as Jesus's birth. He was highly educated and a Pharisee. Initially Paul was a persecutor of Christians. But, while on the road to Damascus to arrest Christians, the risen Jesus appeared to him and commissioned him to take the message of the Messiah to the Gentiles.

Paul was an extraordinary missionary, taking faithful Christians like Barnabas, John Mark, and Silas with him as companions and helpers. He started many churches and preached the gospel of Jesus in Jerusalem, Antioch, Athens, Ephesus, Thessalonica, Corinth, and elsewhere. The book of Acts ends with Paul under house arrest in Rome, welcoming all who visited him and sharing the good news of Jesus.

Paul had an incredible impact on his world—an impact that has continued to this day through his writings. His unique abilities were a valuable asset to God, and he held nothing back from God. All of his training, education, intelligence, and personality were used by God. In Paul, God had a willing servant who gave his all until his last breath.

You might not think you have anything special to offer God, but Scripture says that every believer has a unique set of gifts and abilities that makes them valuable for God's service (1 Corinthians 12:7). Are you willing to let God take your life and all your qualities—and shortcomings—and use them for His service? Or are there some areas of your life that you are holding onto for yourself? You will never know all that God can do through you until you allow Him to have every part of you. Once this happens, Paul's words will come true for you too: "Now to Him who is able to do exceedingly abundantly above all that we ask or think, according to the power that works in us…to Him be glory…forever and ever" (Ephesians 3:20).

A Man Who Battled His Flesh

O wretched man that I am!
Who will deliver me from this body of death?

ROMANS 7:24

Saul was a bright, up-and-coming Jewish religious leader who had been tutored by the great Jewish leader and thinker Gamaliel (Acts 22:3). But a radical change took place in Saul's heart—he met Jesus while on a journey to imprison Christians in Damascus (Acts 9:1-2). From that dramatic encounter onward, Saul, whose name was also Paul, was a devoted follower of Jesus Christ. He went on to have an incredible influence on the early church.

You might think that the great apostle Paul didn't struggle with the fleshly battles that so many of us men face, but you would be wrong. All through his Christian life, Paul experienced ongoing conflict between his sinful flesh and his desire to obey God. He wrote this about his struggle: "I find then a law, that evil is present with me, the one who wills to do good. For I delight in the law of God according to the inward man. But I see another law in my members, warring against the law of my mind, and bringing me into captivity to the law of sin which is in my members. O wretched man that I am! Who will deliver me from this body of death?" (Romans 7:22-24).

Yes, the battle against the flesh is real. But, like the apostle Paul, instead of letting sin master you, you can master it! Here's how Paul did it: "I thank God—through Jesus Christ our Lord!" (verse 25). In another one of his letters, Paul explained how victory is won over sin and the flesh: "Thanks be to God, who gives us the victory through our Lord Jesus Christ" (1 Corinthians 15:57). You cannot win the battle of the flesh unless you stay close to Jesus by reading His Word, seeking His help through prayer, confessing your sin, and avoiding sinful situations and people. The victory is yours and made possible by Christ, but you must do your part.

A Man Who Was Self-Disciplined

Bodily discipline is only of little profit,
but godliness is profitable for all things.

1 TIMOTHY 4:8 (NASB)

The apostle Paul was a gifted and well-educated man. You might assume that these qualities were the reason for his success, and you would be partly correct. But the real reason for his spiritual success was his passionate pursuit of "a crown that will last forever" (1 Corinthians 9:25 NIV). The world is pursuing earthly prizes with bodily discipline, but Paul's motivation was his pursuit of Jesus Christ and a heavenly crown. Paul's disciplined focus had a heavenly perspective, and it made all the difference! The more influence Jesus had on Paul, the more influence Paul was able to have on others.

Paul gave a simple description of spiritual discipline in a letter to his young disciple Timothy: "Train yourself to be godly" (1 Timothy 4:7 NIV). Here are three key characteristics of spiritual discipline:

Effort—"train": The pursuit of any worthwhile goal takes effort. Spiritual growth is not automatic. It requires that you are faithful to be a man of the Word, to pray, and to walk in obedience.

Desire—"yourself": No one can make you grow spiritually. Only you can hunger for self-disciplined training in the ways of God.

Focus—"to be godly": Discipline needs a focus. The athlete focuses on his body. God's man focuses on developing good character. Godliness should be the desire and direction of every aspect of your life.

O man of God, discipline is a good and profitable endeavor. You will not go far without it. Without discipline, you cannot be a man of influence on any level. Make sure your discipline has the right focus. Like Paul, make sure your goal is, first and foremost, to follow God. In fact, that is what Jesus Himself said: "Seek first the kingdom of God and His righteousness, and all these things [the necessities of life] shall be added to you" (Matthew 6:33).

A Man Who Handled Adversity

…in labors more abundant, in stripes above measure, in prisons more frequently, in deaths often.

2 CORINTHIANS 11:23

If you have read anything about church history, you have probably noticed a pattern in the lives of the men and women who were greatly committed to Jesus Christ. All of them experienced great adversity, and many were martyred for their faith. These things were true about the apostle Paul. In fact, Paul faced enormous condemnation for his Christian faith. In a letter to the church at Corinth, Paul listed his sufferings for the cause of Christ: Five times he received 39 stripes, he was imprisoned, beaten, stoned, shipwrecked three times, and faced constant peril from his own countrymen, Gentiles, and robbers (2 Corinthians 11:23-26).

Beyond these external sufferings, Paul prayed three times for God to remove what he referred to as his "thorn in the flesh" (2 Corinthians 12:7). In time, Paul understood that his problems kept him humble, forced him to depend on God, and shaped his character. Paul was able to handle both external and internal adversity because of what he knew about God: "We know that all things work together for good to those who love God, to those who are the called according to His purpose" (Romans 8:28).

Are you suffering from your own particular "thorn in the flesh," whether it's a debilitating illness, a financial reversal, a jealous coworker, an attack on your Christian faith, or a malicious accusation against your character? God understands your pain and has reasons and purposes for your suffering. Turn your "thorn" into trust. Use your situation as an opportunity to trust God and understand what He wants to teach you. As was true about Paul, God's grace is sufficient for you, no matter how great the adversity.

A Man Who Was Teachable

He rebuked Peter, saying,
  "Get behind Me, Satan!
For you are not mindful of the things of God,
  but the things of men."

MARK 8:33

In the biblical accounts of the calling and training of Jesus's disciples, the lists and order of the names of the 12 men who served Him are almost identical. In all four Gospels, the first name in these lists is always Peter. From the day that Jesus first met Peter, he was singled out by Jesus to be a "rock" of strength for the other disciples. He was a natural-born leader and quickly became the spokesman for the group. Yet with all his self-confidence and boldness, Peter had a unique quality that is not often found in a leader of his stature—he was teachable.

Whenever the Lord rebuked Peter for something he said or did, Peter was open to correction. Peter's final exam came after he denied knowing Jesus not just once, but three times. When the resurrected Lord later confronted Peter about this, He didn't ask Peter about his denial. Instead, Jesus asked one simple question: "Do you love

Me…?" (John 21:15). When Peter answered yes, Jesus asked the same question two more times. Peter grieved over his past and his failures, and said, "Lord, You know all things; You know that I love You."

Peter passed his final exam. He had learned his lesson. And Jesus knew His student's commitment was solid and complete. Jesus then gave Peter his marching orders: "Feed My sheep" (verse 17).

Peter's mistakes are vividly portrayed throughout the Gospels. Yet rather than get frustrated and quit, Peter got back up. He used all that he had learned from the Lord to follow the Lord's instructions to feed His sheep.

Follow Peter's example. *Learn* from your mistakes, but *leave* them behind and grow from the process. The key to your spiritual growth and usefulness is your teachability—your willingness to obey your Lord's commands. Learn the principle Peter exemplifies: It's better to be a follower who sometimes fails than one who fails to follow.

A Man Who Gave in Under Pressure

[Peter] said to Him,
"Lord, I am ready to go with You,
both to prison and to death."

LUKE 22:33

Simon, who was named Peter by Jesus, was a fisherman and a native of Bethsaida in the region of Galilee. He and his brother, Andrew, were disciples of John the Baptist until Peter was introduced to Jesus by Andrew. Jesus changed Simon's name to Cephas, which in the local dialect of the day meant "rock," which also translates to "Peter" (Luke 6:14). Peter and Andrew were called by Jesus to become part of His 12 disciples.

A study of the life and character of Peter reveals many noble qualities. His enthusiasm and boldness are traits every Christian should desire. But Peter was just as weak as he was bold, and he often folded and gave in under pressure—as seen in his denials of Jesus and his flight from the agonizing scene of Jesus's crucifixion. Jesus had predicted Peter's denial, but Jesus also said to Peter, "I have prayed for you, that your faith should not fail; and when you have returned to Me, strengthen your brethren" (Luke 22:32).

Aren't you glad God doesn't give up on you when you fail? Peter had great potential, but he often said and did the wrong thing. Yet the God of second chances met him after he had denied Jesus three times and put him back on the road to service. Just as Jesus was ready to forgive and reinstate Peter for usefulness, He is ready to do the same for you. Whatever spiritual failure you might have in your past is an opportunity for you to experience the grace of God.

Maybe you fear that you've failed God one too many times and He won't give you another chance. Well, think again. God knows your heart. And He wants to forgive you and see you back in His service. Go to Him now and receive His infinite love and forgiveness. Your service is needed!

A Man Who Was Asked to Forgive

Having confidence in your obedience,
I write to you, knowing that
you will do even more than I say.

PHILEMON 21

Philemon was a wealthy member of the church in Colosse, a city about 100 miles from Ephesus. Philemon probably became a Christian during Paul's three-year ministry in Ephesus. In God's providence, Onesimus, a runaway slave who belonged to Philemon, had met Paul in Rome and become a Christian.

Paul knew that he had to make sure Onesimus returned to his master, so Paul wrote a letter asking Philemon to forgive Onesimus and welcome him back to serve as a brother in Christ. The purpose of Paul's letter was not to talk about slavery, but forgiveness.

Philemon had Roman law on his side, and Onesimus had indeed broken the law and deserved to be punished. Yet Paul asked Philemon to forgive his slave out of their common love for Christ. We do not know the outcome of Paul's appeal to "do even more than I say," but we do know that Jesus meant for all believers to forgive one another: "For if you forgive men their trespasses, your heavenly Father will also forgive you" (Matthew 6:14).

In the same way that you have been forgiven in Christ, so you too should freely forgive others whether they deserve it or not. Always keep in mind that forgiveness is most Christlike when given to the undeserving. You may also be thinking along with Peter, "How many times should I forgive another person?" Jesus answered this question by saying, "If he sins against you seven times in a day, and seven times in a day returns to you, saying, 'I repent,' you shall forgive him" (Luke 17:4). A willingness to forgive others is an indicator that you too have been forgiven in Christ.

A Man Who Waited on Tables

Seek out from among you
seven men of good reputation,
full of the Holy Spirit and wisdom…
ACTS 6:3

The church at Jerusalem had a problem—a big one! "In those days…the number of the disciples was multiplying" (Acts 6:1). Scholars estimate that the number of men and women in the church at this time could have been close to 20,000. Some were Greek-speaking Jews who had come to Jerusalem for the feasts then later died, leaving behind widows who had no local family or means of support. Philip was one of the seven men selected to take care of these destitute widows. The responsibility of these seven men was to "serve tables" (verse 2).

Even though Philip's assigned task was physical in nature, he was chosen for his spiritual qualities: He was "full of the Holy Spirit and wisdom" (verse 3). Later, persecution erupted, and Philip and many others were forced to flee. Philip went to the region of Samaria, where he eagerly shared the gospel. Through his preaching a revival started up, and many Samaritans became believers. God then led

Philip to meet with an Ethiopian official and explain the gospel. The official, who was returning to his homeland after visiting Jerusalem, also became a believer.

The key to Philip's journey of faith and service was his willingness to obey God. Philip served willingly at any level and any task—from being a servant who waited on widows…to preaching to the despised Samaritans…to leaving a thriving and fruitful ministry in Samaria to go into the desert to talk to one man.

Ephesians 2:10 says you were "created in Christ Jesus for good works, which God prepared beforehand that [you] should walk in them." Like your salvation, God ordained before time began that "good works" should be a part of your life. Like Philip, begin by being a servant, being willing to "serve tables," and tending to those in need at your church. Serving others will help you grow in your faith, and allow your spiritual gifts to bloom. Who knows where God might take you?

A Man Who Did Nothing

Pilate…took water and washed his hands before the multitude, saying, "I am innocent of the blood of this just Person. You see to it."

MATTHEW 27:24

Pontius Pilate was a Roman politician assigned as governor to the region of Palestine. The Jewish people had been a problem from the beginning of Pilate's assignment. Once again, their religious leaders were stirring up trouble—a matter involving a popular teacher who was also supposedly a miracle worker. Pilate questioned this man called Jesus, but found nothing deserving of death. But the pressure from the Jewish religious leaders and the crowds was too great. Pilate chose expediency rather than justice. He made a visual display of removing himself from the process by literally "washing his hands" of what would happen next. Pilate didn't order the death of Jesus, but by choosing supposed neutrality, he was guilty of putting the Son of God to death. He may as well have hammered the nails in Jesus's hands and feet himself!

It is the Irish statesman Edmund Burke who observed, "The only thing necessary for the triumph of evil is for good men to do nothing." That was the message of Jesus's parable of the good Samaritan, in which a priest and a Levite saw a man bleeding and hurt, but chose to do nothing. Only a despised Samaritan stopped and did something. He helped the man in need (Luke 10:29-37).

How often are we tempted to refrain from getting involved, to remain silent and make excuses for not speaking up or sharing our faith? When we say or do nothing, we are still saying and doing something. We are allowing the fear of others to freeze us into inaction. In this way we passively approve of sinful behavior. We become like Pilate, who washed his hands of Jesus, which made way for His death. Ask God today for the courage to speak up for your faith. Stand up for what is morally right, regardless of the consequences. Do something rather than doing nothing!

A Man Who Was Second Choice

Barnabas took Mark and sailed to Cyprus;
but Paul chose Silas and departed.

ACTS 15:39-40

Silas, a Greek-speaking Jew, took part in the Jerusalem Council meeting, during which it was made clear that Jews and Gentiles alike are saved by grace alone. At the conclusion of the meeting, Silas and Judas, who were both prophets, were asked to return to Antioch with Paul and Barnabas to convey this message from the Jerusalem Council. The four of them were to teach the Word and provide encouragement. Judas later returned to Jerusalem, but Silas remained behind and continued his fruitful ministry.

In time, Paul asked Barnabas to go on another missionary trip. Understandably, Barnabas wanted to take his nephew, John Mark, who had abandoned the missionary team in the early days of their first journey. However, Paul objected, so Barnabas took Mark and left for Cyprus. As a fallback, Paul asked Silas to join him. Though Silas was Paul's second choice, he was a strong addition to the team because...

- he was Jewish, which would give him access to the synagogues.

- he was a Roman citizen and would enjoy the same benefits and protections as Paul.

- he was a respected leader in the Jerusalem church.

- he was a prophet and teacher who could help reinforce the message that Gentile salvation was by grace alone through faith alone.

Silas may have been Paul's second choice, but in God's eyes, he was the best choice for what Paul needed. When you become someone's "second choice," remember that "all things work together for good to those who love God, to those who are the called according to His purpose" (Romans 8:28). God knows you, and He knows what you can offer to any situation or task. So when you are chosen, whether second, third, or last, see it as God working for your good and His glory. You have just become God's best choice!

A Man Who Could Wait

There was a man...whose name was Simeon.
and this man was just and devout,
waiting for the Consolation of Israel.

LUKE 2:25

Simeon is introduced early in the Gospel of Luke, after Luke describes the birth of Jesus, the long-promised and long-awaited Messiah. Simeon was described as "just and devout," and he was a frequent worshipper at the temple and a faithful follower of Old Testament prophecies. Simeon had waited his entire life in great anticipation of the coming of the Messiah, the Christ. God honored Simeon's faith and perseverance with a revelation from the Holy Spirit that he would see the Lord's Christ before his death. When Simeon saw the child Jesus and His parents enter the temple, he broke forth in a song of praise, saying, "My eyes have seen Your salvation..." (verses 20-32).

Simeon waited...and waited...and waited for this moment, and sometimes God asks us to wait too. That's the definition of patience—learning to wait. Our natural tendency in today's instant society is to want everything to happen right now. But if you want to be a man after

God's own heart, you need to trust God and let Him set the pace—even if that means waiting.

Waiting is hard, and you might be tempted to "help God out" by manipulating circumstances, but that is never a good option. Instead of rushing forward, walk by the Spirit and be self-controlled or patient (Galatians 5:23). Like Simeon, when you walk with God and strive to be "just and devout," God's Holy Spirit will give you the ability to wait—to wait for that medical condition to improve, that hoped-for transfer to come through, that prodigal child to return, and for whatever else concerns you. In the meantime, while you are waiting, do useful and positive things that bring you closer to God, like praying and finding help and nurturing yourself in His Word. You will be glad you did, and God will bless you for being willing to wait.

A Man Who Was Full of the Holy Spirit

[Stephen], being full of the Holy Spirit, gazed into heaven and saw the glory of God.
ACTS 7:55

Being first at something is usually a good thing, like being the first person in space, or the first person to break the four-minute mile. For Stephen, however, his "first" was being the first martyr in the church's long line of people killed for their faith.

Because Stephen was of "good reputation, full of the Holy Spirit and wisdom," he was one of seven men chosen to supervise the distribution of food to the widows in the Jerusalem church (Acts 6:3). The book of Acts describes Stephen as a man who was full of God's grace and power, and full of faith.

What you are—your godly character—is more important to God than what you do for Him or anyone else. God wants your obedience more than your service. That's what the prophet Samuel told King Saul after he had disobeyed God. Samuel said, "Behold, to obey is better than sacrifice" (1 Samuel 15:22).

Before you busy yourself in service to God, make sure you are fully yielded to Him. Then your service will be empowered by Him. As Stephen began his speech before he was executed by stoning, the Jewish religious leaders "saw his face as the face of an angel" (Acts 6:15). Like Stephen, as you yield to God's leading you will be calm, unruffled, composed, reflecting the presence of God. You will be a graphic testimony to the life-changing power of God to an unbelieving world.

A good reputation. Full of the Holy Spirit. Full of wisdom. God's Word will tutor you in these spiritual qualities and build them into your soul as you walk in love and obedience to your Lord and Savior.

A Man Who Doubted

Unless I see in His hands
the print of the nails...
I will not believe.

JOHN 20:25

Thomas was one of the original 12 disciples who had followed Jesus and been taught by Him for three years. These trusted men were selected to serve as representatives of Jesus during His earthly ministry (Matthew 10:2-4). Thomas was the disciple who asked Jesus, "Lord, we do not know where You are going, and how can we know the way?" (John 14:5). He asked this immediately after Jesus had said He was going to "prepare a place" for them (verse 3).

But Thomas is most known for expressing doubt that Jesus had actually been raised from the dead. During Jesus's first appearance to the apostles, Thomas had been absent. Eight days later, Jesus suddenly appeared again while Thomas and the others were cloistered in a room with the doors shut. Jesus didn't rebuke Thomas for his unbelief; instead, He compassionately offered Thomas proof of His resurrection. Thomas's immediate response was, "My Lord and my God!" (John 20:28).

Doubt is not unusual when it comes to spiritual things. Even in the very presence of Jesus, the disciples had doubts about who He was. Jesus called His disciples men of "little faith" (Matthew 16:8). We can almost understand Thomas's doubt: Resurrection from the dead? How could that be possible? But ultimately, doubt must make a choice. When it comes to Jesus, there is no middle ground.

When you catch yourself struggling with any doubts about Jesus and what He expects of you, admit your doubts to God, and begin looking for answers in the Bible. Take this plea of a perplexed father and make it your own: "Lord, I believe; help my unbelief" (Mark 9:24).

A Man Who Was to Train Others

The things that you have heard
from me among many witnesses,
commit these to faithful men
who will be able to teach others also.

2 TIMOTHY 2:2

The New Testament speaks of a disciple in Lystra named Timothy (meaning "honored by God"). Timothy was the son of a Jewish woman who was a believer, and a father who was a Greek. He was well spoken of by those in the churches in Lystra and Iconium.

The apostle Paul was impressed by Timothy's character qualities and wanted him to travel with him during his missionary journeys. Paul referred to Timothy as a "fellow worker," a "beloved and faithful son in the Lord," one who was "like-minded" to Paul, and "a true son in the faith" (Romans 16:21; 1 Corinthians 4:17; Philippians 2:20; 1 Timothy 1:2). Paul wrote several of his letters with Timothy present. He also wrote two letters directly to Timothy while Timothy pastored the church at Ephesus, instructing him about leaders and their behavior in the church. Paul was deeply fond of Timothy and valued him immensely as a coworker in spreading the gospel.

Paul's investment in Timothy helps us to remember the importance of training the next generation of godly men. Paul was a trainer of men. He mentored and sent out many, including Timothy. Paul knew that his one life would eventually be over, so he did what he could to raise up men like Timothy, who would go on to teach and train others in the faith.

Are you following in Paul and Timothy's footsteps? Are there "Timothys" you are training to be the next generation of on-fire Christian men? Start with your children— your daughters, who need training in godly behavior, and your sons, who need training toward being godly men, husbands, and fathers. In the same way that Paul passed the baton of faith on to Timothy, you are responsible for helping to prepare the next generation—to "go therefore and make disciples" (Matthew 28:19).

A Man Who Was Reliable

If anyone inquires about Titus,
he is my partner and fellow worker...

2 CORINTHIANS 8:23

The apostle Paul was a gifted and highly motivated servant of Christ. But he knew that the work of planting and maturing churches could not depend on any one personality. Others had to be trained to assume the roles of building, encouraging, and discipling other believers. Titus was one of the young men trained by Paul to carry on the ministry after he was gone.

Titus proved to be an able assistant to Paul. For example, as he matured in the faith, Titus was given the assignment of settling the difficult issues that erupted in the church in Corinth. Then as Paul's life drew to a close, Titus was left in Crete to oversee all the churches on the island and to appoint and train leaders. And in his letter to Titus, Paul wrote that he was sending replacements so Titus could meet him at Nicopolis in Greece (Titus 3:12).

Paul had so much confidence in Titus that when Titus went on a mission, it was as if Paul was going himself. Paul told the church at Corinth, "Thanks be to God who puts the same earnest care for you into the heart of Titus" (2 Corinthians 8:16). As a result of his loyalty and reliability, Titus had a profound impact on the early church. Because of his influence, the churches under his care took root and grew. Titus was a strong and dedicated servant Paul could rely on for many critical tasks.

How about a reliability check? Can others in your church or in your workplace count on you to do what you say you will do? Be where you say you will be? Arrive when you are supposed to—even early? Faithfulness and reliability are hallmarks of spiritual maturity. You can have a great influence in your church, on the job, at home, and in your community by being reliable—a person who people can depend on.

A Man Who Was Trusted

When I [Paul] come, whomever you approve...
I will send to bear your gift to Jerusalem.

1 CORINTHIANS 16:3

As the apostle Paul retraced his steps on his final missionary journey and visited the churches he had planted on an earlier trip, men were selected from each local church to accompany him on his return to Jerusalem. Trophimus was the man chosen from one of these churches in Asia. He was tasked to carry an offering from his church to help the church at Jerusalem. The selection of Trophimus indicates he was a man of high moral character who could be trusted with this great honor and privilege. As Proverbs 25:13 tells us, "Like the cold of snow in time of harvest is a faithful messenger to those who send him, for he refreshes the soul of his masters." We know Trophimus fulfilled this responsibility because he was again mentioned as being with Paul in Jerusalem (Acts 21:27-29).

Trust takes a lifetime to be gained, but can easily be lost with just one unfaithful act. Trust, or trustworthiness, is a foundational quality for a man after God's own heart to possess. Another term for this quality is integrity. A person with integrity can be trusted to do the right thing for the right reason, even when no one is watching.

The apostle Paul saw the Christian life as a stewardship and wrote, "It is required of stewards that one be found trustworthy" (1 Corinthians 4:2 NASB). How trustworthy are you? If your church and its leaders were looking for a trustworthy man for an important job, would your name be on the list for consideration?

Trust is also an important character quality needed in secular workplaces. Can your employer count on you to get the job done? To do the work required? Ask God to make you a trustworthy man who can be counted on to do what is asked, whatever the cost, for the glory of God (1 Corinthians 10:31).

A Man Who Was Dependable

Tychicus, a beloved brother, faithful minister,
and fellow servant in the Lord,
will tell you all the news about me.

Colossians 4:7

We first meet Tychicus while he was traveling with the apostle Paul on the way to Jerusalem (Acts 20:4). Paul continued on to Jerusalem, completing his final missionary journey, whereas Tychicus seems to have been left to minister at Miletus (Acts 20:15,38). Tychicus is not mentioned again until Paul's first imprisonment. Both Colossians and Ephesians refer to Tychicus as bringing news about Paul's condition while the apostle was in prison.

Tychicus provided faithful help and service to Paul. He carried messages to and from the churches and represented Paul to others. While Paul was gifted to preach, teach, and write, Tychicus demonstrated the priceless quality of simply being a reliable helper—of serving others. Paul was able to send Tychicus on any task, confident that he would be a dependable, faithful messenger and get the job done.

The church, the body of Christ, is an amazing organism. Paul described its functions this way: "There are diversities of gifts, but the same Spirit. There are differences of ministries, but the same Lord. And there are diversities of activities, but it is the same God who works all in all" (1 Corinthians 12:4-6). Each believer is given a different spiritual giftedness "for the profit of all" (verse 7).

You don't have to be the man who preaches and teaches to be of significant use to your church. Like Tychicus, every church needs helpers—helpers who are committed, trustworthy, honest, and reliable. Be a man people can count on, a man who stands out as being reliable. Follow in Tychicus's footsteps, and be faithful in all things.

A Man Who Wanted to See Jesus

He sought to see who Jesus was,
but could not because of the crowd,
for he was of short stature.

LUKE 19:3

Who doesn't love a parade, unless you are too short to see *what*—or, as in the case of Zacchaeus, *who*—is passing by? Zacchaeus was not only a tax collector, but a chief tax collector, which indicates he probably supervised a large district of other tax collectors. This explains his great wealth. It's interesting to note that a short time earlier, Jesus had encountered a rich young ruler, and after their discussion, Jesus declared, "How hard it is for those who have riches to enter the kingdom of God!" (Luke 18:24).

Thankfully, Zacchaeus had the right response when he met Jesus. As the Lord walked by and saw this little man perched on the branch of a tree, trying to get a glimpse of Him, Jesus invited Himself to have lunch in Zacchaeus's home. Zacchaeus then offered to "give half of my goods to the poor; and if I have taken anything from one by false accusation, I restore fourfold" (Luke 19:8). Zacchaeus's willingness to make restitution was proof that his conversion was genuine. It was the fruit, not the cause, of his salvation.

The difference between the rich young ruler and Zacchaeus was the condition of their hearts. One "became very sorrowful" (Luke 18:23), but Zacchaeus "received [Jesus] joyfully" (Luke 19:6). Jesus knew Zacchaeus's heart as well as he knew the man's name—and he knows you and your heart too. Have you eagerly sought out Jesus? And have you joyfully accepted Him as your Savior? Then as happened with Zacchaeus, "salvation has come to [your] house" (verse 9)!

Now it's your turn to seek out others who want to see and know Jesus. They won't see the physical Jesus, but they will see you, His ambassador. Be bold and speak up, because all believers "are ambassadors for Christ, as though God were pleading through us: we implore you on Christ's behalf, be reconciled to God" (2 Corinthians 5:20).

A Man Who Was Blameless

*They were both righteous before God,
walking in all the commandments and
ordinances of the Lord blameless.*

LUKE 1:6

Many people appear righteous in the public eye, and especially at church. They profess faith in Christ and perform outward activities of godliness. But sadly, inwardly they fail the true test of godliness, forgetting that "the LORD does not see as man sees; for man looks at the outward appearance, but the LORD looks at the heart" (1 Samuel 16:7).

Meet Zacharias. This man—and his wife—had a heart for God and walked with God on a daily basis. The Bible says Zacharias walked "in all the commandments and ordinances of the Lord blameless" (Luke 1:6). This man didn't pick and choose which laws and ordinances he would obey—he chose to obey all of them! In other words, Zacharias was obedient to follow all the commands of Scripture. With this sincere, sold-out-to-God lifestyle, Zacharias would qualify as a New Testament elder

222

or leader who must be "blameless" (1 Timothy 3:2) or "above reproach" (NASB).

Do you take time to know God's Word so you can obey it? So you can accurately apply it to your life? God made being "blameless" a requirement for His leaders in the New Testament church. Since being "blameless" is possible, how can you develop a strong commitment to God? Here are some basic guidelines that you should want as part of your daily life:

- Develop a "first things first" mentality and read your Bible first thing every day.

- Communicate daily with God by praying about everything, not just your latest crisis.

- Attend church to worship and grow in your knowledge of the Word.

- Team up with mature men in the church who can encourage your spiritual growth.

- Avoid people and places that pull you away from living God's way (1 Corinthians 15:33).

JESUS, THE GREATEST MAN WHO EVER LIVED

A Man Who Was Both God and Man

In the beginning was the Word,
and the Word was with God,
and the Word was God.

JOHN 1:1

Who is the greatest single figure that the world has ever produced? The Jews would say Abraham or Moses. Muslims would say Mohammed. Buddhists would say the Buddha. The Chinese might say Confucius. But without a doubt, the greatest person who has ever lived was Jesus of Nazareth. The Bible tells us Jesus was more than a man—He was also God. Jesus not only created the world, He also became a man so He could be the Savior of mankind by willingly dying on a cross as the perfect sacrifice to pay the penalty for people's sins (1 Corinthians 15:3-4).

What does the life, death, and resurrection of Jesus mean to you? Many people merely acknowledge the fact that Jesus was a person, and continue on with their life without giving Him another thought. But if the Bible is true in what it says about Jesus, then those who do not accept Him as Savior will face Him at the great white throne judgment, where they will answer for the sins they committed in this life (Revelation 20:12).

The other option is to…

- acknowledge Jesus as God,
- acknowledge that you are a sinner in need of forgiveness, and
- accept Jesus's sinless death on the cross as the only acceptable sacrifice for the payment and forgiveness for your sins.

If this is the option you chose, you are now a new creation, with the Spirit of Jesus indwelling you. You have the power for godly living moment by moment as you follow in Jesus's footsteps and keep His commandments. With Jesus as your Savior, you will want to praise and thank Him every single day for your new life—your eternal life!—in Him.

A Man Who Had an Impact

Go therefore and make disciples...
MATTHEW 28:19

Jesus was born of a virgin named Mary, who was betrothed to Joseph from Nazareth. An angel commanded Joseph to name Mary's child Jesus, meaning "the Lord is Salvation" or "Savior" because He would save people from their sins. Jesus, equal to God, entered our world to dwell among us and become the sinless sacrifice that would deliver people from their sin.

Jesus began His three-year earthly ministry when he was about 30 years old. He performed many miraculous acts of healing and demonstrated His power over the forces of nature and the spiritual realm. Jesus often communicated His teachings through parables or stories about everyday occurrences that taught important life lessons.

How was it possible for Jesus to have such a colossal impact on the world when He lived for only 33 years and taught for such a short time in one small area of the globe? The answer? Discipleship. Jesus took a small band of 12 ordinary men and, in three years, He trained them and turned them into a force that shook the very foundations of the world. These common men were empowered by God's Spirit and took the message of Jesus's resurrection and His offer of forgiveness for sin to the ends of the earth.

Jesus told His followers to go and make disciples, and only a true disciple of Christ can do this. Wherever you live and work, these actions and choices will help you to impact the lives of others:

Mirror Jesus's heart and message in your conduct.

Follow Jesus without hesitation.

Take Jesus's message into the world, as His disciples did.

Extend Jesus's forgiveness to others.

Live in a way that draws others to Jesus.

Be available to spend time with others who also desire to be Jesus's disciples.

A Man Who Was Filled with Wisdom

Render therefore to Caesar the things that are Caesar's, and to God the things that are God's.

MATTHEW 22:21

Everything has a source...except God. God is the source of all things, including wisdom. His wisdom and knowledge come from no one (Job 21:22). This means that when Jesus, God in human flesh, walked the face of the earth, perfect wisdom was on display for all to behold. When confronted with trick questions that were seemingly impossible to answer, Jesus gave responses that confounded his enemies. For example, when asked why the Jewish people should pay taxes to the despised Roman government, Jesus answered, "'Render...to Caesar the things that are Caesar's and to God the things that are God's.' When [the people] heard these words, they marveled, and left Him and went their way" (Matthew 22:21-22).

Would you like to have wisdom? The ability to correctly apply what you know? That's the definition of wisdom, and the starting point for your quest is God: "The fear of the LORD is the beginning of wisdom, and the knowledge of the Holy One is understanding" (Proverbs 9:10).

As a believer, your starting point to knowing God is reading and studying your Bible. That's where you will discover the "knowledge of the Holy One." And any time wisdom is required (which is always), you only need to ask for it: "If any of you lacks wisdom, let him ask of God, who gives to all liberally and without reproach, and it will be given to him" (James 1:5).

God promises you wisdom, but you must seek it. Wisdom calls, but you must answer. Wisdom is available, but you must use it. You also cannot count on yesterday's wisdom for today's needs. When you wake up tomorrow, seek fresh wisdom through prayer and time in God's Word. Do this for the rest of your life, and you will become a man who is wise.

A Man Who Was a Servant

The Son of Man did not come to be served, but to serve, and to give His life a ransom for many.
MARK 10:45

People around the world, both Christians and non-Christians, in the past and present, agree Jesus was a great person. And yet Jesus never wrote a book. He never commanded an army of soldiers. He never moved people to revolt. What did Jesus do that has caused people around the globe to acknowledge for centuries that He was the greatest man of all time, the greatest man who ever lived? What made Him so great?

In a very few words, He served others. Jesus's example and message of servanthood has been passed on to us with this command: "through love serve one another" (Galatians 5:13).

Do you struggle with the idea of serving others? As a guy, do you think being a servant is not a very manly quality? Yet Jesus Christ was a servant—the greatest one who ever lived. His mission was "to serve, and to give His life a ransom for many." When there's a need, don't wait to be asked to help, or wait for someone else to do it. Like

Christ, you can decide that you, too, will act whenever you see a need or something that needs to be done.

Open your heart. Open your eyes. And open your hands. But most of all, look to Jesus. He came to earth with a different lifestyle and a radical life message. He defined true greatness as serving others (Matthew 20:26). And He lived out that definition. His mission was to serve others and to give His very life away.

Today, Jesus is asking you, as His follower, to follow His example:

to be like Him,

to develop a servant's heart,

to help others, and

to start with those who live under your roof—your family.

A Man Who Promised Rest

Come to Me, all who are weary and heavy-laden, and I will give you rest.

MATTHEW 11:28 (NASB)

Jesus was a constant irritation to the religious leaders of His day. For centuries these leaders had added numerous man-made requirements to the law—the Scriptures God gave to Moses in the first five books of the Old Testament. These religious rules and regulations caused the people to be "weary and heavy-laden." In short, they were worn out, and pleasing God seemed hopeless.

Jesus invited His audiences—and you too—to "Come to Me…and I will give you rest." Jesus offers spiritual rest, deliverance from fear and despair, and freedom from the guilt that comes from a works-based religion. Jesus's rest also offers continual guidance and help from the Holy Spirit, and ultimately, eternal rest in heaven. But there is one condition: You cannot know this rest until you heed Jesus's invitation to "Come to Me."

Are you enjoying spiritual rest through a personal relationship with Jesus Christ? If so, this peace and rest that you now possess will be experienced more fully in heaven.

But what about physical rest? Jesus fully understood the need for this as well. To His worn-out disciples He said, "Come aside by yourselves to a deserted place and rest a while" (Mark 6:31). They had just returned from an especially grueling time of ministry, and Jesus wanted to take them away from the crowds for some much-needed physical rest. Jesus also knew what was coming next on the disciples' hectic schedule—the feeding of 5,000 hungry souls (verses 33-44).

For you to have a balanced and effective Christian life, both spiritual and physical rest are necessary. Do your part by making sure you get physical rest, because God has important spiritual work for you to do in His service!

A Man Who Provides True Worth

Do not fear therefore;
you are of more value
than many sparrows.

MATTHEW 10:31

Jesus spent three years teaching and training His disciples. Because there were so many who hated Jesus, the disciples were fearful of those who might want to harm them. Jesus understood their fears and assured them of the Father's watch-care. He said, "Do not fear those who kill the body but cannot kill the soul" (Matthew 10:28), and then He told them of their worth to God. If God valued even the most insignificant of birds—sparrows—how much more did He value His own children?

Some people suffer from a low self-image because they erroneously think they aren't worth anything. Others have the opposite problem—they have a huge ego. They think they are worth everything! Both groups of people have their focus on themselves and their abilities or lack of them.

As a Christian, your worth does not come from your abilities, but from your relationship to Jesus Christ. He said, "He who abides in Me, and I in him, bears much fruit; for without Me you can do nothing" (John 15:5).

You may have some physical limitations, but God has not made any mistakes. He has created you, and you are "fearfully and wonderfully made" (Psalm 139:14). He has also given you worth in Christ.

No matter what your limitations, thank God for each one of them. Your limitations force you to trust God and depend on Him and His strength in the areas in which you are weak. As God said, "My strength is made perfect in weakness" (2 Corinthians 12:9). You may not be successful from the world's perspective, but when you abide in Christ, you will bear "much fruit" (John 15:5).

A Man Who Was Thankful

*Father, I thank You
that You have heard Me.*

JOHN 11:41

After being rejected by the people in Nazareth (Matthew 4:13), Jesus shifted His headquarters to the town of Capernaum, still in the region of Galilee. He performed many wonderful miracles in and around this area. Wouldn't you think the people would have enthusiastically embraced Him as Messiah? Yet they showed complete indifference to Him. Jesus denounced their rejection and specifically singled out Capernaum (Matthew 11:20-24). But then He did something unexpected. Rather than being downcast, He offered up thanks to His Father: "I thank You, Father, Lord of heaven and earth, that You have hidden these things from the wise and prudent and have revealed them to babes" (verses 25-26). Notice what Jesus thanked and praised the Father for:

- hiding the significance of His words and works from those who were supposedly "the wise and prudent."

- that He had chosen to reveal Him and His message

to "babes" instead of the "wise," to those who were not highly educated, but humble and willing to receive the truth.

Jesus possessed an attitude of thankfulness in the midst of negative circumstances. That He was thankful is truly amazing because, as the Son of God, He created and owned everything! Even so, Jesus never failed to demonstrate a thankful spirit to His heavenly Father.

Has anything happened in your life that seemed odd or didn't make sense? Maybe you are struggling to understand how a loving God could let something terrible happen to you or a loved one. If so, you are not alone. Many people wonder why God has allowed certain things to happen. Rather than question God with your whys, learn from Jesus's example and be thankful. As the Bible says, "In everything give thanks; for this is the will of God in Christ Jesus for you" (1 Thessalonians 5:18).

Books by Jim George

10 Minutes to Knowing the Men and
Women of the Bible
The 50 Most Important Teachings of the Bible
The Bare Bones Bible® Handbook
The Bare Bones Bible® Handbook for Teens
The Basic Bible Pocket Guide
A Boy After God's Own Heart
A Boy After God's Own Heart Action Devotional
A Boy's Guide to Discovering His Bible
A Boy's Guide to Making Really Good Choices
A Dad After God's Own Heart
A Husband After God's Own Heart

Know Your Bible from A to Z
Knowing God Through Prayer
A Leader After God's Own Heart
A Man After God's Own Heart
A Man After God's Own Heart—A Devotional
The Man Who Makes a Difference
One-Minute Insights for Men
You Always Have a Friend in Jesus for Boys
A Young Man After God's Own Heart
A Young Man's Guide to Discovering His Bible
A Young Man's Guide to Making Right Choices

Books by Jim & Elizabeth George

A Couple After God's Own Heart
A Couple After God's Own Heart Interactive
Workbook

God's Wisdom for Little Boys
A Little Boy After God's Own Heart
Through the Bible One Rhyme at a Time

To learn more about Harvest House books and
to read sample chapters, visit our website:

www.harvesthousepublishers.com

HARVEST HOUSE PUBLISHERS
EUGENE, OREGON
